TORAFU ARCHITECTS
IDEA + PROCESS
2004 - 2011

TORAFU ARCHITECTS
IDEA + PROCESS
2004 - 2011

トラフ建築設計事務所の
アイデアとプロセス

美術出版社

I would describe Torafu's work as a deliciously perfumed and delightfully presented melt-in-the-mouth dish with the right amount of spice and an unforgettable aftertaste. Seeing the degree of ease with which they can achieve this result using materials at hand is truly impressive. When I commission a job, I like to refrain from giving constraining instructions as I prefer to be pleasantly surprised by the result—a very rare treat for a work giver. Mr. Suzuno is a quiet man without a hint of boastfulness. He dutifully listens to our concerns and patiently dispels any doubts we might have on a presentation and I find myself mesmerized at how his logically exposed concepts can make us take to radically new ideas.

Their work involves a great amount of behind-the-scenes planning and verification that often goes unnoticed, but the models shown to us successfully reveal all the possibilities contained in these creative seeds.

I believe their breadth of mind comes from their elaborate preparations and their confidence comes from their originality. Their tremendous hard work is what gives them the edge to continue reshaping space to their will like a virtuoso. I hope they will continue to prove, that it is realizing unconventional ideas as if it were nothing that is able to change the times, and I hope for them to be in the vanguard for many years to come.

Akira Minagawa

Born 1967. Founded "minä" (now "minä perhonen") in 1995. With his brand of timeless craftsmanship, Minagawa has aimed to create clothes that illuminate your everyday life and heighten your spirits every time you wear them. In the same spirit, he has sought to express handcrafted designs through textiles, a stance he has adopted since the brand's inception, earning him numerous invitations from art galleries abroad and at home. Minagawa has held exhibitions in the Dutch city of Tilburg in 2009 and at Spiral Garden in Aoyama, a trendy neighborhood of Tokyo, in 2010.

FOREWORD

トラフの仕事は盛り付けが楽しく香りの良いスパイスの効いた口どけの良い、さらに後味で隠し味がのぞく一皿料理の様だと思っている。

それをつくっている当人はさも身近な材料でササッとつくりましたみたいに普通に振舞っているのが印象的。依頼する私たちはやりたいことを伝える。「ああやって、こうやって」を言うのが勿体ないと思うからだ。どんな答えを出すのか楽しめる依頼はめったにない。鈴野さんの佇まいは静かだ。口八丁な素振りは一切ない。プレゼンテーションへの私たちの反応をゆっくり解釈するかの様に耳を傾けてくれる。アイデアの説明は理にかなった筋道のあるもので見たこともない様なアイデアもすっと気持ちに入ってくるから不思議だ。

この仕事の仕方は見えないところにある膨大な検証と試作に裏打ちされたものに違いない。持ってきてくれる模型からたくさんの可能性について試行した痕が見えてくる。下ごしらえをしっかりしているからゆとりがある。誰とも似てないから自信がある。そんなトラフはこれからも空間を自在に料理していくのだろう。常識ではないことを当たり前の様にさりげなくするということが、時代をスルリと変えていくことをこれからも証明し続けて欲しい。

皆川 明

1967年生まれ。1995年に「minä（現 minä perhonen）」を設立。日常の暮らしに光を当て、身に着けるたび気持ちが高揚する服づくり、時の経過により色褪せることのないものづくりを目指している。設立以来一貫して手作業で描く図案をテキスタイルとして表現する姿勢から、国内外の美術館で展覧会への招聘も多い。2009年にオランダ・ティルブルグにて、2010年に東京・青山のスパイラルガーデンにて展覧会が開催された。

CONTENTS / 目次

4   FOREWORD by Akira Minagawa / 皆川明によるまえがき

CHAPTER 1

FORM THAT CREATES ACTIVITY　動きを誘発するかたち

14   TEMPLATE IN CLASKA / テンプレート イン クラスカ
18   HOUSE IN OOKAYAMA / 大岡山の住宅
24   NIKE PRESSROOM / NIKE PRESSROOM
28   Yuichi Yokoyama Solo Exhibition at KAWASAKI CITY MUSEUM / 川崎市市民ミュージアム「横山裕一」展
32   Pappa TARAHUMARA "PunK・Don Quixote" / パパ・タラフマラ「パンク・ドンキホーテ」
36   minä perhonen arkistot / ミナ ペルホネン アルキストット
40   Kitchen Blocks / キッチンの積み木

CHAPTER 2

THE POWER OF A SINGLE IDEA　ワンアイデアが持つ力

44   HOUSE IN KOHOKU / 港北の住宅
52   Y150 NISSAN PAVILION / Y150 NISSAN パビリオン
58   Light Loom (Canon Milano Salone 2011) / 光の織機 (Canon Milano Salone 2011)
64   HermanMiller Store Tokyo / ハーマンミラーストア東京
68   SPINNING OBJECTS / 回転体
72   EXHIBITION UNDERGROUND / 地下展 UNDERGROUND
76   HOUSE IN NAKAMARU / 中丸の住宅
78   TORANOANA AKIHABARA / とらのあな AKIHABARA
79   EGG ZABUTON / エッグ座布団

80   **COLUMN 01**   THE SOURCE OF TORAFU'S IDEAS / **コラム01** トラフのアイデアソース
86   PROFILE / プロフィール

CHAPTER 3

MATERIALS AND GRAPHICS　素材とグラフィック

88   NEW PEOPLE / NEW PEOPLE
94   Exhibition of minä perhonen / ミナ ペルホネンのエキシビション
96   3M store / 3Mストア
98   yozakura (Kaneka Milano Salone 2011) / yozakura (Kaneka Milano Salone 2011)
102 GREGORY TOKYO STORE / GREGORY TOKYO STORE
104 NIKE 1LOVE / NIKE 1LOVE
110 CARBON HOLDER / 炭素ホルダー
110 SKY HOUSE / スカイハウス

CONTENTS

CHAPTER 4

SUGGESTIONS FOR AN OFFICE SPACE　オフィススペースへの提案

- 112　NIKE JMC / NIKE JMC
- 120　1-10design Kyoto Office / 1→10design 京都オフィス
- 124　KAYAC Ebisu Office / 面白法人カヤック 恵比寿オフィス
- 126　UDS Shanghai Office / UDS上海オフィス
- 130　DWJ Office / DWJ Office
- 134　**COLUMN 02**　TORAFU AND MATERIALS / **コラム02** トラフと素材

CHAPTER 5

A DESIGN ORIGINATING FROM A CONNECTION　かかわりから生まれるデザイン

- 140　Run Pit by au Smart Sports / Run Pit by au Smart Sports
- 146　INHABITANT STORE TOKYO / INHABITANT STORE TOKYO
- 150　EXHIBITION LIFE AND LIGHTING / くらしとあかり展
- 152　EXHIBITION "minä perhonen + torafu new / study" / ミナ ペルホネンとトラフの新作 / 習作
- 156　CHELFITSCH" FREETIME" / チェルフィッチュ「フリータイム」
- 158　TABLE ON THE ROOF / テーブル オン ザ ルーフ
- 162　Deck / デッキ

CHAPTER 6

TURNING THE MINIMUM INTO THE MAXIMUM　最小限を最大限に

- 164　BOOLEAN (Tokyo University Tetsumon Cafe) / ブーリアン (東京大学医学部教育研究棟 鉄門カフェ)
- 168　EXHIBITION "bones" / 「骨」展
- 172　HOUSE IN INOKASHIRA / 井の頭の住宅
- 174　RING PARKING / リング パーキング
- 176　KIRIKO BOTTLE / キリコ ボトル
- 177　CMYK / CMYK
- 178　tapehook / tapehook
- 180　airvase / 空気の器
- 185　**COLUMN 03**　TORAFU AND TOKYO / **コラム03** トラフと東京

- 190　[Intent]-[Author]=[Story] Text by Jun Aoki / 〈作為〉-〈作者〉=〈ストーリー〉 寄稿 青木淳
- 194　PROJECT DATA + DRAWINGS / 作品データと図面

1

**FORM THAT
CREATES ACTIVITY**

動きを誘発するかたち

Form that affects people's behavior and awareness.
What is it about form that enriches our environment?

人の行動や意識に働くかたち。
かたちがまわりを豊かにするというのは
どのようなことなのか。

FORM THAT CREATES ACTIVITY

TEMPLATE IN CLASKA
テンプレート イン クラスカ / 2004

A planar solution was utilized to make guests feel comfortable in the reduced 18m² room, whereby functional elements and furniture such as the closet, desk and chair were built into the wall.

18m²という小さな部屋をリノベーションするにあたり、その狭さを意識しないように、できるだけ単純な操作を行うことが重要と考えた。クローゼット、デスク、イスといった家具的な要素も壁面に埋めこみ、平面的に解決した。

TEMPLATE IN CLASKA

A Wall to Arrange Items

An old hotel was renovated in Meguro, Tokyo and reopened as CLASKA in September 2003. For the project, we were approached to design three rooms for long-term guests.
Part of the project brief was to include in each room an AIBO, a pet robot produced by Sony, and artwork by three Japanese artists.
The first step in the design process was to focus on all necessary items in the room including the art work, AIBO, room furniture and guest's belongings. Since they are of all different sizes and shapes, we proposed to use a piece of thin wall with laser cut holes as a TEMPLATE to display these items.
It's not that the paintings or the AIBO are of more importance, but by taking goods and furnishings to which we would otherwise pay no attention to, and putting these into a frame, we have treated these elements equally. At the same time, it became possible for the template wall to hold the intensity necessary to define the whole space.

要素を並列させる壁

東京・目黒の老朽化したホテルをリノベーションし、2003年9月にオープンしたホテル「クラスカ」。いくつかある客室のうち、長期滞在者のための3室の改装を手掛けた。
各部屋それぞれにアーティスト3名による絵画を掛けること、ロボットペットの「アイボ」を各部屋に設置することが条件として要求された。
そこで、絵画、アイボ、ホテルの備品や宿泊者の持ち物など、さまざまな形や大きさの物を、ゆるやかに規定するために、"テンプレート"（型板）をモチーフにした、穴を穿った1枚の薄い壁を提案した。
絵画やアイボが特別であるのではなく、むしろ自分の持ち物や備品など普段気にもとめない物に対しても、額縁に入れて飾るような操作を施すことで、要素を並列に扱った。一方で、切り取られたテンプレートの壁面が空間を決定する強度も併せ持つこととなる。

The wall conceals the inner structure, giving the room an uncluttered feel.
入口から見る。壁面は、既存の構造躯体を見せずに、室内をすっきり感じさせるためでもある。

Storage areas behind slits in the wall hold CDs, DVDs and remote controls, while speakers are hidden behind the "hair dryer's blow" pattern.

壁に収納することによって、まったく性質の異なる要素をフラットに扱える。スリットにはCD・DVDソフトを入れたり、リモコンを差し込むことができる。「ドライヤーの風」の部分はスピーカー。

Indirect lights in the wall provide most of the lighting in the room.

照明はできる限り壁面からの間接照明としている。

The template wall was executed by laser. (top)
"テンプレート"の壁面はレーザーカットで加工された（上）。

The wall was divided into eight parts with consideration to strength and workability. The blocks were carefully mounted to enhance the accuracy before being reassembled at the hotel. (bottom)
壁面の内部は、強度や施工性を考えて、八つのブロックに分節されている。工場でつくられたブロックは精度出しのため一度組み立てられたのち、バラして現場へ搬入し、再度組み立てられる（下）。

FORM THAT CREATES ACTIVITY

HOUSE IN OOKAYAMA

大岡山の住宅 / 2010

Individual rooms and the common area are divided by the centrally-located entrance hall.
中央の玄関ホールを挟んで、個室とパブリックスペースに分割している。

HOUSE IN OOKAYAMA

The various rooms are connected by differently designed staircases that seem to weave through the gaps between rooms.
積み重ねられた諸室の間を縫うように、意匠の異なる階段で接続。

FORM THAT CREATES ACTIVITY

The living room on the 2F looking back towards the stairs. Since the floors are not divided, the presence of family can always be felt. (top left)
2階のリビングを階段側に見返す。階で分断されていないため、別の部屋にいても家族の気配が感じられる（左上）。

The 2F kitchen is placed between the wing walls that support the whole structure. Utilizing the wooden boards as shelves or as desk space creates a large wall storage area. (top right)
構造を担う袖壁の間に納まるキッチンカウンター。板をかけ渡し、棚やデスクとして使うことで、構造体を利用した大きな壁面収納としている（右上）。

The elevated floor turns into a desk in the bedroom that is 700mm below the level of the living room floor. (bottom left)
リビングから700mm床レベルが下がった寝室では、張り出した床が机になる（左下）。

HOUSE IN OOKAYAMA

A Collection of Large Furniture

This is a wooden, three-story duplex located in a residential district of Tokyo. The site, consisting of a 4.7m frontage area with a length of 16.5m, is long and narrow and is adjacent to buildings on three sides except for the north side where it faces a road. Making the most of these conditions, careful consideration was given so that the narrowness of the frontage area would not feel narrow at all. In order to get rid of a tight hallway space, the entrance hall and stairway are placed at the center, dividing the bedrooms and public spaces into north and south. The configuration, in which each and every room stacks like large furniture, blurs the boundary between architecture and furniture. The cross-sectional design achieved here gives an impression of freedom when compared to the floor configuration of a typical residential building.
Through an additional process that treats every component of this residence like a customizable piece of furniture, ample margins have been created for changes to be made after moving in. The residence itself is an object that is continuously transforming.

大きな家具の集積

東京の住宅地に建つ木造3階建ての二世帯住宅。敷地は間口4.7m、奥行き16.5mという細長い形状で、周囲三方に建物が近接、北面のみ道路に面している。この条件を活かしながら、間口の狭さを極力感じさせないよう配慮した。間口をさらに狭めてしまう廊下をなくすため、中央の玄関と階段が、南北に寝室とパブリック空間とを分割する平面計画としている。
それぞれの部屋が大きな家具のように積み重なるという構成は、建築と家具との境界をあいまいにして、一般的な建物の階層を感じさせない自由な断面計画を実現させた。
住宅の各要素を家具として扱う付加的な操作によって、施主の入居後も手を加えられる余白が生まれ、この住宅自体が常に変化を受け入れる器となる。

A bay window that also serves as a bench offers more breadth of space between the wall and ceiling.
天井と連続する壁面側にはベンチにもなる出窓を設けて、空間に広がりを与えている。

FORM THAT CREATES ACTIVITY

The 1F living room. This room features a 150% higher ceiling, reaching the middle storage room visible on the upper right.
1階のリビング。1.5層分の天井高があり、右上に見えるのは中間の収納部屋にあたる。

The entranceway is visible from the 1F kitchen for the grandparents.
1階にある親世帯のキッチンから玄関方向を見る。

HOUSE IN OOKAYAMA

A long cross-section model. In this configuration, each room overlaps so that floors become indistinct. A 1.4m high box-shaped storage room has been inserted between 1F and 2F to accommodate the owner's large number of personal possessions.

長手断面模型。階を明確に分けず、各室を積み重ねた構成。持ち物が多いため、1階と2階の間に高さ1.4mの収納部屋を挿入。

The roof materials extend down the outer surface of the walls as though the roof were like a hat. (left)

屋根材を外壁面まで伸ばし、帽子のように屋根をかぶせた外観（左）。

The interphone and mailbox for the two generations feature the owner's trademark as a motif incorporated into the wall surface. (right)

二世帯分のインターホンとポストは、施主のトレードマークをモチーフにして壁面に組み込んだ（右）。

FORM THAT CREATES ACTIVITY

NIKE PRESSROOM

NIKE PRESSROOM / 2007

A Continuous Space Layout

We were approached to design a NIKE pressroom in the basement of a building requested to function as a branding area, a meeting room and a styling room. The site also needed to be open and large enough to hold events in without giving off the feeling that it is located in a basement.
To fulfill these conditions, we found a way to make every room function independently without being cut off from others. We set up virtual vertical layers to partition the entire space at 1000mm intervals, and secured volumes by clipping certain portions of the planes from these layers.
The partitions make it impossible to see beyond the spaces they surround, thus separating every room. While these partitions block direct gazes, the rooms continue into each other through openings along the layers.

連続する空間の仕切り

既存の建物の地下1階に計画したNIKEのプレスルーム。ブランディングエリア、ミーティングルーム、スタイリストルームなどの各機能に加え、イベント時には全体を大きく使えるニュートラルな空間が要求された。また、地下を感じさせないようなオープンな印象の場所であることも求められた。
そこで、たくさんの部屋が機能的に独立しつつも、連続するような空間の仕切り方を模索した。まず一方向に1000㎜の間隔で仮想の垂直面をレイヤー状に立てていく。その仮想面の一部を切り欠くことで、必要な部屋のボリュームを確保した。
視線はレイヤー状の面の直交方向には閉じられ、面に沿った方向にのみ開放される。視線の方向によって人や商品が見え隠れし、閉じながらも連続する空間を生み出した。

Layers partition the space at 1000 mm intervals all the way to the back where the NIKE "Swoosh" sign looms.
1000㎜ごとに空間を横断する壁面が連なる。何重にも縁取られながら、最深の壁面に浮かび上がるNIKEの「スウッシュマーク」。

FORM THAT CREATES ACTIVITY

We used 36mm thick veneered partitions on which Manchurian Ash is agglutinated on the surface; white colored glass walls and mortar floors coated in 3mm clear resin.

レイヤー状の面は36mm厚のタモ練り付け材を使用。他の壁面には白色のカラーガラス、床面はモルタルに3mmの透明樹脂コーティングを施した。

NIKE PRESSROOM

The lobby area is fitted with sofas and tables for meetings. (top)

エントランスロビーにあたるエリア。ミーティングテーブルや待合のソファなどが置かれる（上）。

Materials were limited to wood, concrete and glass, standing as a neutral background to people and merchandise. (bottom left)

木、コンクリート、ガラスと素材を限定し、人や商品の背景として中立的な存在とした（左下）。

Cut out panels extending above from wall to wall serve as display fixtures. (bottom right)

切り欠かれた面は、空間全体を横断して壁面まで到達し、展示のための什器として使用できる（右下）。

FORM THAT CREATES ACTIVITY

Yuichi Yokoyama Solo Exhibition at KAWASAKI CITY MUSEUM
川崎市市民ミュージアム「横山裕一」展 / 2010

A Track Table That Follows a Body of Work

This exhibition space design project is for Yuichi Yokoyama's first large-scale solo exhibition. Yokoyama is an artist with a painting background who discovered manga as a form of expression to create original works of art.
The site's characteristic curved wall inspired us to design a track-and-field-like exhibition space where visitors complete laps by following the sheer number of drawings placed along the track. The manga reading direction conducts visitors on the inside to move in the opposite direction to those on the outside. This arrangement brings visitors together to share reading from the same displays, allowing for momentary interactions as they move past one another. The semi-directive line of flow allows for a simplified route and selective movement to coexist on the same track.
By using furniture with an artificial and industrial feel straight out of the artist's manga and having visitors move in succession through the pages, we strived to create a space that exudes an overall impression attuned to Yuichi Yokoyama's vision.

作品を追いかける トラックテーブル

絵画を学んだのち、漫画を表現手段に独創的な作品を生み出している横山裕一の大規模な初の個展。その会場構成のプロジェクトである。
膨大な量の原画を順に鑑賞できるよう、会場の特徴的な曲面壁を活かし、陸上競技のトラックのような形状を持つ展示台による平面計画とした。展示台の外周、内周で展示作品を分け、ページを順に追いながら"トラック"を周回する。漫画を読む方向に合わせて、外周と内周で人の動く方向が逆向きとなるため、対向する鑑賞者とはすれ違うときだけ対面する。半強制的な動線でありながら、順路の単純化と選択的な動きが許容できるようにしている。
ページを追って鑑賞者がぞろぞろと行進する風景や、作中の人工的で工業的なシーンから抜け出してきたような家具などで、会場全体の印象が横山裕一の世界観と呼応する空間を目指した。

Yuichi Yokoyama Solo Exhibition at KAWASAKI CITY MUSEUM

The artificial lawn strips covering the exhibition floor are rolled up at one end to serve as benches while the dry brushing sound of footsteps resonate with the sound-effects and perspective on nature expressed in his work.

床全面に敷いた人工芝は、作品で表現される人工的な自然観に共鳴する。床面は歩くたびに「ザッザッ」という乾いた音を発し、作中で多用される擬音を実際に体感できるようにした。また、その芝の一部を巻き取ってベンチとしている。

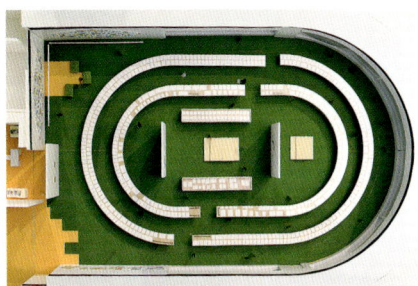

The track-and-field themed exhibition site model.
会場の模型。全体が陸上競技のトラックのような構成をしている。

An open space where visitors can interact with the artist at work.
会場の一角に設けられた公開制作のスペース。机が置かれ、作品づくりとともに、来場者との対話も図られた。

The site Kawasaki City Museum features a 600m² open area where visitors can appreciate his early art works and all the storyboards from his most representative manga; "New Engineering", "Travel" and "NIWA". (p.28)

会場となった川崎市市民ミュージアムの展示室は、仕切りのない約600㎡の空間。初期の絵画作品と漫画作品の代表作である『ニュー土木』『トラベル』『NIWA』の膨大な量の原画すべてを、順に鑑賞できる (p.28)。

Yuichi Yokoyama Solo Exhibition at KAWASAKI CITY MUSEUM

Facing the center screen are benches made with wooden crates and pallets from the museum, creating an impression of engineering structures in the artist's work.
中央には映像を鑑賞するためのベンチが置かれる。ミュージアム所有の積枠や木箱を利用しており、作中の土木的な構造物をイメージさせる。

FORM THAT CREATES ACTIVITY

Pappa TARAHUMARA "PunK·Don Quixote"
パパ・タラフマラ「パンク・ドンキホーテ」/ 2009

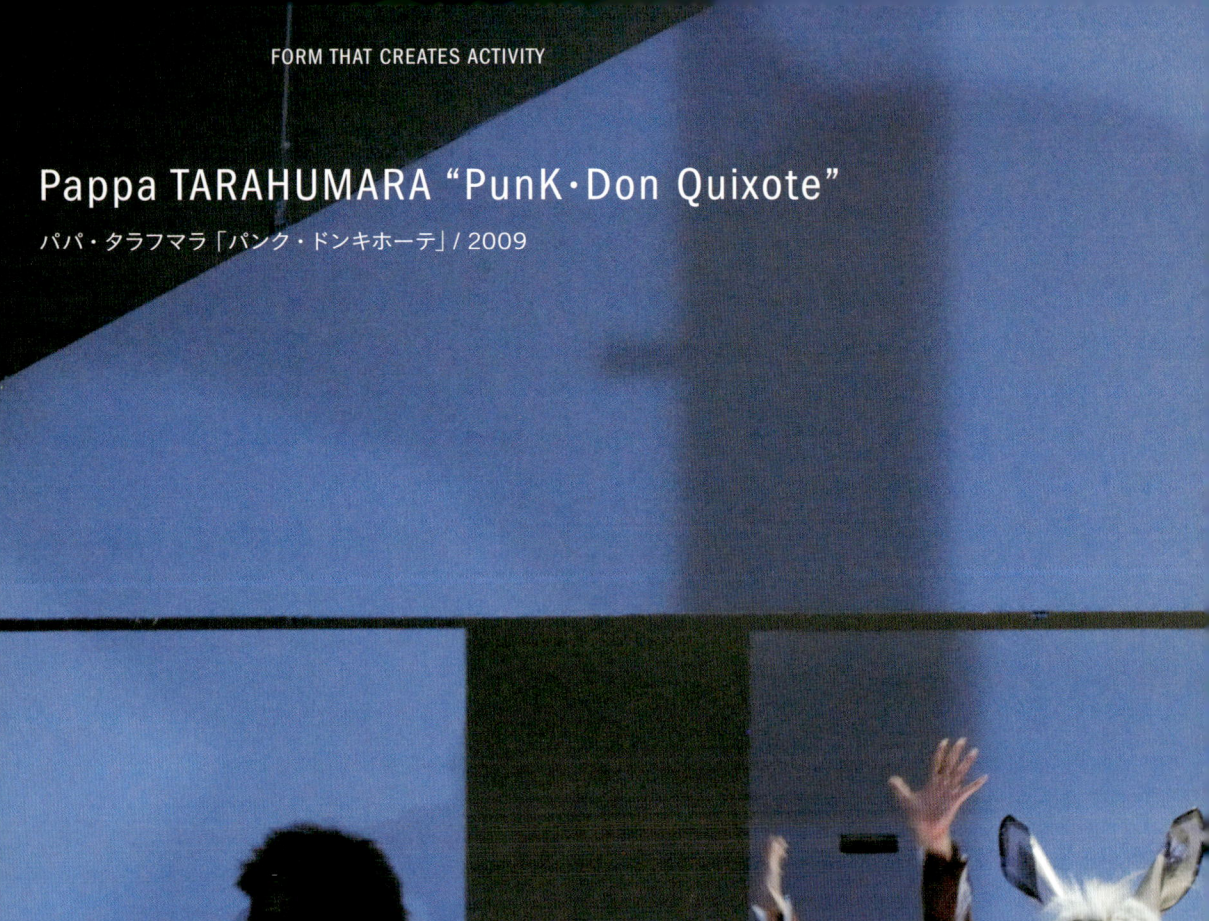

Pappa TARAHUMARA "PunK·Don Quixote"

The Morphing and Collapsing Shape of a House

Hiroshi Koike, founder of Pappa TARAHUMARA, asked us to build a stage set for the company's production: PunK·Don Quixote. His work is a mixture of theater, musical performance and dance that often defies categorization, and thus we proposed a stage that does not stand still as a mere background but gradually morphs and follows the play dynamically.
The play portrays a patriarch consumed by delusions and his family. While it visits contemporary problems, it does not do so in a pessimistic way but also brings about a bright touch filled with hope. We were requested to propose a stage set with a house whose white walls would decay over time, echoing the family's own disintegration.
Parts of the structure are turned around, moved or removed altogether from where they belong, causing it to gradually lose its purpose as a house. The whole stage and its disarticulated parts become an integral part of the performance.

変容、崩壊する家のかたち

小池博史主宰のカンパニー、パパ・タラフマラの公演「パンク・ドンキホーテ」の舞台美術を手掛けた。パパ・タラフマラの舞台は、演劇なのかミュージカルなのかダンスなのか、またはそのどれでもないとも言える。芝居の背景という静的なものにとどまらない、徐々に変容していく動的な舞台を求められた。
奇怪な妄想にとらわれた父親を持つ家族たちの物語。現代の問題に触れながらも、悲観的ではなく希望を込めた明るさを伴っている。崩壊していく家族、それを象徴する白い家型が徐々に崩れていく舞台セットを提案した。
家を形成していたパーツは、物語の進行に従って、もとの位置から外れ、方向を変え、または舞台から姿を消し、家としての意味を失っていく。舞台背景は道具に分解され、舞台上のパフォーマンスに取り込まれる。

FORM THAT CREATES ACTIVITY

Since Pappa TARAHUMARA's stage lights are never lowered to accommodate stage rearrangements, a great deal of thought and concern went to ensure performers' actions in one scene would set the stage for the next in a transitioning manner.

The end offers a completely different view to the spectator where roles between humans and their strange creatures have been reversed. The play culminates with this shocking portrait as the house and its household lay in ruins.

Pappa TARAHUMARA "PunK·Don Quixote"

パフォーマーが一つの動きをしながら、次のシーンのための布石を打ちつつ動けるよう意識して細部を考えた。それはパパ・タラフマラの舞台が暗転しないことに起因する。つまり、セットを組み替える場面はなく常に動き続けることを意味する。

物語の最後には、舞台はまったく違う様相と化す。いつの間にか、人間とそれ以外の奇妙な動物との主従関係が逆転してしまう物語の進行ともあいまって、もとの家型がなくなってしまうという衝撃的なクライマックスを迎える。

minä perhonen arkistot

ミナ ペルホネン アルキストット / 2010

A Free Space That Incorporates Change

This is an interior project for fashion brand minä perhonen's new store. "Arkistot" means "Archive" in Finnish, and this word symbolizes the concept of the store, which deals in items they have released in the past. We proposed a store unlike any other where products change fluidly, defying seasons and conventions.
The space has the depth of a typical row house where we placed mobile box-shaped displays of varying height and size to accommodate changing store layouts or events such as workshops. Removable shelf boards and hangers can be reconfigured to avoid restricting the arrangement of items.
Each piece of furniture presents a mirror and a blackboard surface. Facing various directions, the mirrors catch hidden angles and create a complex image of the surroundings, which confers expanse to the space. A space with the freedom to accommodate change, and one which allows items in the archive to be looked at from a new point of view.

変化を受け入れる自由な空間

ファッションブランド、ミナ ペルホネンの新店舗の内装計画。店名の「アルキストット」とはフィンランド語で「アーカイブ」を意味し、過去に発表したアイテムを扱うことに由来する。そのため、通常の店舗と異なり、シーズンに縛られず、商品は流動的に変化する。その変化に対応するような空間を提案した。長屋のように奥行きのある空間に、高さと大きさの違うボックス型の可動什器を点在させた。レイアウトの変更やワークショップなどのイベントにも対応する。また棚板とハンガーラックも取り外し、移動できることで商品の陳列が制限されないよう配慮している。各什器はそれぞれミラー面と黒板面を持ち、さまざまな方向を向くミラー面は、振られる角度によっても、複雑に周囲を映し込んで空間に広がりを与える。アーカイブのアイテムと新たな視点で向き合え、変化を許容できる自由な空間を目指した。

minä perhonen arkistot

The 2F and 3F of this three-story building make up the store. This is a view of the 2F section that mainly handles clothing. (p.36)

3階建てのビルの2、3階が店舗。洋服をメインに扱う2階の全景 (p.36)。

The 3F has shelves to store and display textiles that have been showcased in the past.

3階には過去に発表されたテキスタイルを収納、陳列できる棚を設置。

FORM THAT CREATES ACTIVITY

Depressions in the existing structure's floor, normally considered a disadvantage, are covered with epoxy resin to create a white pattern that accents the store interior.
通常デメリットとなってしまう既存躯体の床の凹みにエポキシ樹脂を流してできた白い模様が、アクセントとなって店内を演出する。

The drawings on the blackboard are regularly updated to provide a fresh impression on every visit. (p.39 top)
黒板面に描かれるドローイングが更新されることで、訪れるたびに新鮮な印象を与える (p.39上)。

A strangely non-directional rhythm is produced by painting parts of furniture items displaying an irregular edge. (p.39 bottom)
什器の小口を不規則に見せ、一部を塗装することで方向性のない不思議なリズムを生む (p.39下)。

minä perhonen arkistot

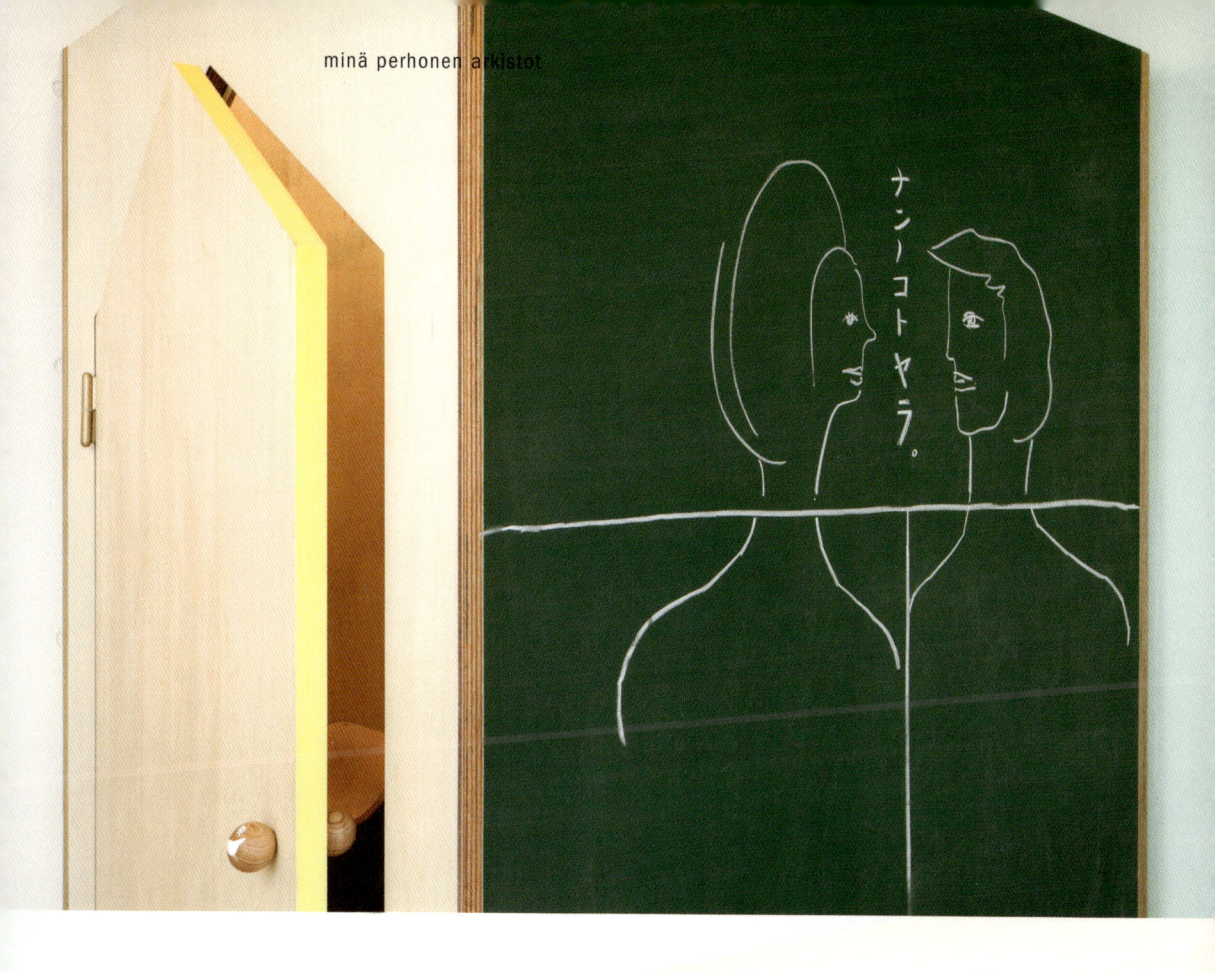

FORM THAT CREATES ACTIVITY

Kitchen Blocks
キッチンの積み木 / 2010

40

Kitchen Blocks

FORM THAT CREATES ACTIVITY

Wooden Blocks That Make the Dining Table More Enjoyable

Kitchen tools in the shape of blocks. Space was created inside the blocks so that they could be utilized as a salt and pepper case, toothpick case, bottle opener, chopstick rest, coaster, pasta measure, and kitchen timer. The daily dinner table experience becomes more enjoyable with these blocks when it seems as though one is playing with them. These were produced in parallel with the "more trees Exhibit – Feel the Forest over 12 Days" (Roppongi Axis Gallery) exhibition that showcases the activities of "more trees" and their reforestation project.

食卓を楽しくする積み木

積み木の形をしたキッチンツール。積み木の中に空間を設け、ソルト＆ペッパーケース、楊枝入れ、栓抜き、箸置き、コースター、パスタメジャー、キッチンタイマーとして使えるようにした。積み木で遊んでいるような風景が、毎日の食卓を楽しくする。
森林再生プロジェクトに取り組むmore treesの活動を伝える展覧会「more trees展 森を感じる12日間」(六本木AXISギャラリー)にあわせて製作された。

Block-shaped kitchen tools made with thinned wood from hinoki cypress trees. There is a salt and pepper case, toothpick case, timer, etc. (top)
ヒノキの間伐材でつくられた積み木形のキッチンツール。それぞれがソルト＆ペッパーケース、楊枝入れ、タイマーなどになっている（上）。

The 12 blocks are made to be stored in a square box whose outer case measurements are W217×D217×H50mm. (bottom)
12個の積み木が正方形の箱に収まるようになっている。外箱のサイズは、W217×D217×H50mm（下）。

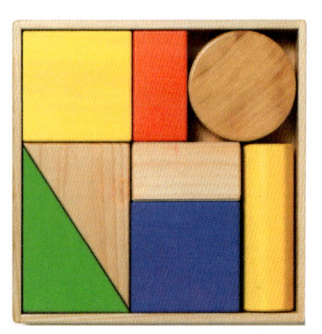

2

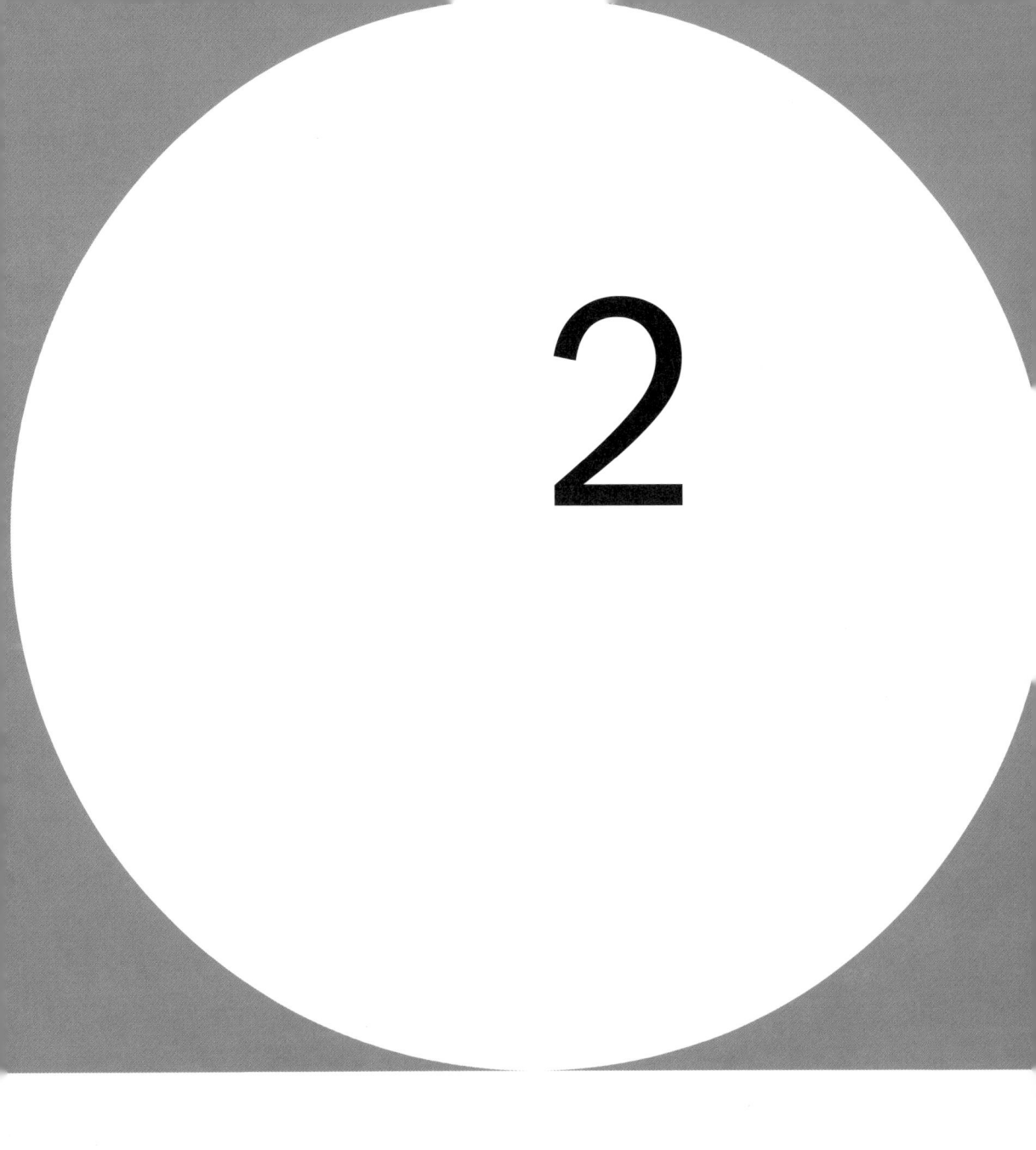

THE POWER OF
A SINGLE IDEA
ワンアイデアが持つ力

A single idea that has come to fruition under various conditions confers diversity and integrity.

さまざまな条件から生み出された一つのアイデアが全体を覆いながらも、多様性を持たせている。

THE POWER OF A SINGLE IDEA

HOUSE IN KOHOKU

港北の住宅 / 2008

The shape of the roof clearly appears on the inside. As opposed to the concrete exterior, the inside of the house is given a white finish where light and shadow interplay.

屋根の形状がそのまま反映された室内。コンクリート素地の外部とは対照的に、白塗装による仕上げとし、光と影の変化を映し込む。

HOUSE IN KOHOKU

The Roof Stretching Towards Light Shapes the Interior and the Exterior

This site is located in a quiet residential region on a hill in Yokohama. The client, a married couple who has lived in this area for a long time, wanted a small but sunny one-story house.
Because the neighboring houses are lined very close together, the site is sloped to the north, and the neighboring house to the south is two-storied and built on a higher tiered ground, it is rather difficult to let in light from the south. We designed tube-shaped roofs facing various directions that let in light through glass located at the top, which protects privacy at the same time.
The shapes and ridges of these tubes clearly appear on the inside of the house, which seamlessly separate the living space. Thus the particular roof shape has an overall impact on the interior of this one-story house and it was our aim to make the exterior and the interior appear as two sides of the same object We decided to use 150mm reinforced concrete to capitalize on the roof structure in a rational manner, thereby making it possible to obtain an interior space void of pillars.
The roof not only lets in light and drains rainwater but also gives a moderate separation on the space inside. The brightness and softness of light differs according to the season and the time of day, which in turn changing the look of the place.

光を求める屋根が内外をつくる

横浜の高台にある閑静な住宅地。施主の夫婦は長く住み慣れたこの場所に、小さくも明るい平屋の住居を希望した。
敷地は、住宅が密集した北向き勾配の斜面で、ひな壇状に高い南側隣地は2階建ての建物があり、南からの採光は期待できない。個々にトップライトを持つ異形の筒状の屋根が方々を向くことで、プライバシーを保ちながら光を採り入れる計画とした。
一方、この形がダイレクトに現れる室内では、折板状の稜線が空間を柔らかく分節する。屋根形状が室内空間全体に影響する平屋の特徴を活かし、内部と外部が同時に成立するような空間を目指した。
筒形屋根の折板効果を合理的に扱えるようRC造としたことで、室内に柱が出ず、コンクリートの厚みも一律150mmで構成できる。
光を採り込み、雨水を受け流す屋根が、内部では空間を過度に分節し、季節や時間によって差し込む光の表情や明るさの違いでその場所を変容させる。

THE POWER OF A SINGLE IDEA

The roof, akin to a collection of acorn barnacles, takes in light by avoiding the buildings in the vicinity. The site has the form of a flagpole and interfaces with the street in a trimmed fashion.
フジツボが集まってできたような筒形の屋根が、隣地の建物を避けて光を採り込む。敷地はいわゆる旗竿形で、細いアプローチを通じて道路と接している。

HOUSE IN KOHOKU

The view on the bedroom from the living room is mitigated by the roof ridges.
リビングから寝室を見る。適度に視線を遮る天井の稜線。

THE POWER OF A SINGLE IDEA

View of the living room and bedroom from the kitchen. On the left is a wooden volume infixed in a space where the ceiling is highest. The wet areas are contained inside while a loft on the top of the volume is used as an office for the client's son.

キッチン側から寝室、リビングの方向を見る。左手の最も高さのある空間には、木造のヴォリュームを入れ子状に設け、その内部を水回り、上部をロフト状の小部屋とした。ロフトは独立した息子が仕事場として使う。

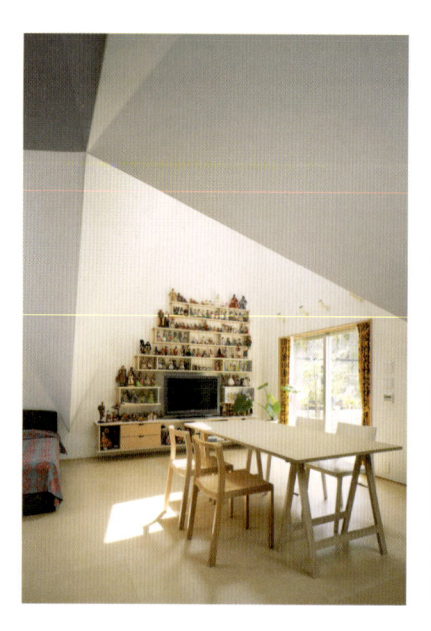

Living / dining room with access to the garden. While the necessities of life are all found close to each other, the roof ridges keep an adequate separation between them.

庭に面したリビングダイニング。衣食住が近接しながらも、天井の稜線がその間に適度な距離感を保つ。

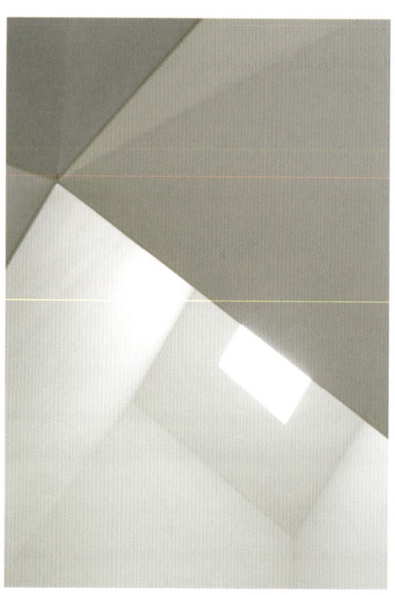

Interior view of the roof. Light enters differently through each one of the four tubes.

天井を見上げる。4本の筒ごとに光の入り方が異なる。

HOUSE IN KOHOKU

Since the floor and built-in furniture are made of medium-density fiberboard with a paint finish, the furniture looks as if it has grown from the floor.
キッチンと玄関の方向を見返す。造り付けの家具の素材は染色したMDFで、同材である床から派生したように見える。

THE POWER OF A SINGLE IDEA

Setting up the concrete casts for the reinforced concrete frame. The flimsiness of unfinished panels remind us of the set of a play.
コンクリートの型枠を組み立てる。施工中は型枠パネルのペラペラ感が舞台美術のような印象を与える。

Placing the last piece of the inner cast.
内部型枠最後の1枚を施工中。

The moment we removed the cast, we felt the light pour in.
型枠の外れた状態。光が差し込むことを実感できた瞬間。

HOUSE IN KOHOKU

The interior's soft character offers a contrast against the exterior's concrete persona.
外観のコンクリートの表情とは対照的に内部は柔らかい表情を持つ。

THE POWER OF A SINGLE IDEA

Y150 NISSAN PAVILION
Y150 NISSAN パビリオン / 2009

Y150 NISSAN PAVILION

Using Air as a Material

The "NISSAN Y150 Dream Front Pavilion" was designed as part of the EXPO Y150 initiative commemorating the 150th Anniversary of the opening of the Port of Yokohama. The Nissan Motors PR project spanned two areas targeting children and focused on the theme of environmental communication with "Word Park" and "Pivo Labo". "Word Park" is a large exhibition space that houses 16 giant bubbles ranging from 4.5 to 10m in diameter, inviting visitors to playfully navigate through them. Images projected on the bubbles take the form of its spherical contour, giving the impression that these virtual images have become real. We designed a site populated by these bubbles, and that help materialize the space between them. Stemming from Nissan's vision for a future with clean air, we envisioned a space permeated with light and used the presence of air as a material.

空気という素材

横浜港の開港150年を記念するイベント「開国博Y150」。そのパビリオンの一つ「NISSAN Y150 ドリームフロジト」の会場構成。二つの展示室(「コトバパーク」、「ピボ・ラボ」)での、日産自動車の環境活動コミュニケーションと、子どもを対象とした企画内容に適した空間が求められた。
コトバパークでは、直径4.5〜10mの大小16個の気泡(バルーン)で大きな展示室を満たした。訪れた人は気泡の余白を縫うように回遊する。気泡の球面には湾曲した像が映り込み、虚像が実体化(物質化)したような印象を与える。その気泡(図)を会場全体に充填するように配置して、余白(地)を実空間として計画していった。
クリーンな空気へのまなざしを持つ日産のメッセージから、空気そのものを素材の一つとしてとらえ、光や気配の浸透する空間を目指した。

"Word Park", located in an exhibition space on the Shinko Pier, Port of Yokohama. The transparent and opaque bubble membranes blend in the light and the shadows cast by visitors.
横浜の新港埠頭にあるイベント会場内に設けられた展示室コトバパーク。気泡の膜は透明なものと不透明なものがあり、通り過ぎていく人影や差し込む光を球状の境界面が拾い上げる。

THE POWER OF A SINGLE IDEA

Y150 NISSAN PAVILION

The floating spheres touch at certain points, supporting each other and creating a feeling of tension. (p.54)
気泡同士は点で接し合い、支え合うような緊張感を保ちながら浮遊する(p.54)。

The bubbles can be illuminated by stepping on the generators.
足踏み式の発電装置で、気泡内に設置された照明を点灯させることができる。

THE POWER OF A SINGLE IDEA

Messages written by children on cards shaped like leaves tumble inside several of the bubbles during the exposition. The messages were gathered over the course of the exhibition.

いくつかの気泡は、葉っぱの形をしたメッセージカードを宙に舞い上げる仕組みを備える。メッセージは会期中に蓄積されていく。

Looking out to "Word Park" from "Pivo Labo". "Pivo Labo" features the Nissan PIVO2 electric car and a video showcase of the company's environmental practices, which can be viewed from sitting on seats made of paper honeycombs.

ピボ・ラボからコトバパークを見る。ピボ・ラボでは、電気自動車「PIVO2」の展示と日産が取り組む環境活動の映像が流され、ペーパーハニカム製のイスで鑑賞できる。

Y150 NISSAN PAVILION

The bubbles are made of two kinds of membranes: white and transparent. They were brought in folded before being hung from the ceiling. Keeping the feeling of tension in between the hanging bubbles required a strict arrangement.
白色、透明2種類の膜でできた気泡をたたんで搬入し、天井から吊す。球体が接していることで生まれる、余白の緊張感を維持するため、設置位置が厳密に調整された。

An air-enveloping chair is made by expanding honeycomb paper.
ハニカム構造の紙を広げて空気をはらんだようなイスをつくる。

The model of the exhibition space. Its large volume is filled with spheres.
会場の模型。大きな気積の空間が球体で充填される。

THE POWER OF A SINGLE IDEA

Light Loom (Canon Milano Salone 2011)
光の織機（Canon Milano Salone 2011） / 2011

Light Loom (Canon Milano Salone 2011)

THE POWER OF A SINGLE IDEA

The "luminous flux screens" extend across the 15.5m space, where as many as 20,000 pieces of strings were used in total. The word "WONDER" can be seen reflected from the projection wall.

15.5mに渡って空間を横断する光束スクリーン。糸の数は2万本におよぶ。投射面には「WONDER」の文字が、反転して見えている。

Light Loom (Canon Milano Salone 2011)

Spectators can not only take in the projected images, but look back at the light source, which reveals the same images reflected on the strings.

観覧者は通常の投射先の映像だけではなく、光源側を振り向くことで、次々と糸に映し出されていく光の像を見ることができる。

Screens of Air

As part of the 50th year anniversary of the "Milano Salone", we were invited to design the Canon exhibition. The installation, designed to the theme of "NEOREAL WONDER", was to include the application of the company's digital imaging technology. We were influenced by how light, normally formless, can appear as "light forms" before the spectators' very eyes when dust is illuminated in the dark. We wanted to build a new relationship with light, so by tracing the radiating light beams with countless strings, the light is artificially given substance. Density of the strings creates the image screens that stretch across the space. These string screens differ from the traditionally flat screens as it can take on a variety of expressions. A new reality could be experienced through the mysterious unity of light and images, blending inside a space that was neither virtual nor real.
The word "WONDER" was set up on the entrance wall as though it had been woven together by the countless strings on the reverse side. These are the strings that appeared to capture the constantly moving light, weaving it inside the space.

空気のようなスクリーン

50周年を迎えた「ミラノサローネ」における、キヤノンの展示会場構成。「NEOREAL WONDER」をテーマに、同社のデジタルイメージング技術を駆使した新しい映像空間が求められた。
暗闇のちりが照らされて"光の形"が見えるように、もともと姿形を持たない光が目の前に現れるとき、光との新しい関係を築くことができると考えた。
放射状になった光の形を無数の糸でトレースすることで、光を擬似的に実体化した。糸がつくる錐体は、その線密度によって映像スクリーンとなって空間を横断する。糸によるスクリーンは、従来の平面的なものとは異なり、さまざまな表情を見せる。光や映像が空間に溶け込んだかのような不思議な一体感によって、虚構とも現実ともつかない、新たなリアリティーを体感できる。
エントランス壁面には「WONDER」の文字が、その裏側の無数の糸で編んだかのように設えてある。糸が絶え間なく動く光をとらえ、空間に織り込んでいるように見える。

Light Loom (Canon Milano Salone 2011)

After completing the experience and returning to the entrance, visitors can find the word "WONDER" woven on the wall.
体験を終え、エントランスに戻ってくると「WONDER」の文字が編み込まれていることに気づく。

The image tunnel that extends from the entrance to the main space.
エントランスからメイン空間に至る映像のトンネル。

In order to see how the images would reflect on the radiating strings, we carefully carried out repeated simulations.
放射状の糸の束に映像がどのように映し出されるかを見るため、丹念な検討を繰り返した。

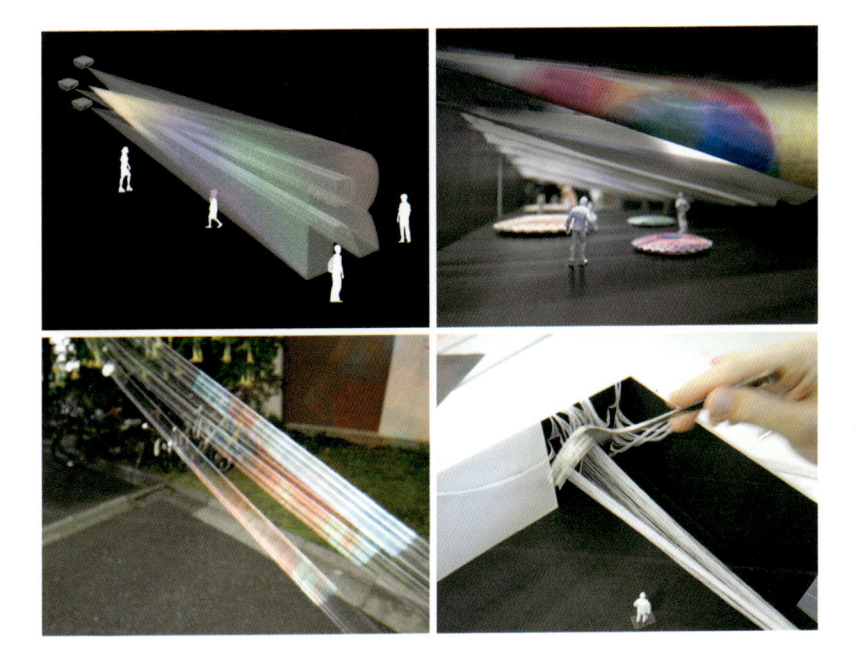

THE POWER OF A SINGLE IDEA

HermanMiller Store Tokyo

ハーマンミラーストア東京 / 2010

A Space Reminiscent of the Lightness of a Park

The world's first Herman Miller road side store was designed to showcase products by renowned designers and promote wider brand awareness to the general public.
Taking in the Marunouchi site and its immediate environment into account, we proposed a space that could be enjoyed with the same ease as taking a stroll through a park. Like picnic blankets spread out in the park, a great variety of materials cover the floor, allowing customers to experience various situations by moving products around while adding color to their surroundings. Like a park that allows many different uses every day, the store layout can easily be changed through this flexible system to create a fresh impression on customers every time they visit.
We envisioned this flagship store design to hold events that can communicate a perpetually renewing image that incorporates Herman Miller's heritage.

公園のような気軽さを感じさせる空間

世界初となるハーマンミラーの路面店の計画。著名デザイナーの作品を取り扱うハーマンミラーを幅広く認知させ、一般客を意識したストアとなることが求められた。
計画地である丸の内の周辺環境を踏まえ、公園のような気軽さを持って訪れることのできる空間を提案した。公園で敷物を広げてピクニックを楽しむように、床面に配された多種多様な素材は、空間に彩りを与えるとともに、製品を移動させるとさまざまなシチュエーションでの検討が可能になる。この店内レイアウトの変更が容易なフレキシブルなシステムは、日々自由な使われ方を許容する公園のように、来店のたびに新鮮な印象を与えることができる。
旗艦店となるこのストアで、ハーマンミラーのバックグラウンドを保ちながらも、イベント性にあふれ、常に新しいイメージを発信できるような場所を目指した。

HermanMiller Store Tokyo

Aluminum frames were used to cover the existing ceiling, giving an impression of the shades of trees.
既存天井をアルミのフレームで覆い、木陰のように演出した。

THE POWER OF A SINGLE IDEA

The mobile furniture units, which seem to be protruding from the surface of the floor, make it easy to change the store layout and is also utilized to create stages during events and seminars.

床面が隆起したような可動什器は、店内のレイアウト変更を容易にし、イベントやセミナー時の演台としても使用される。

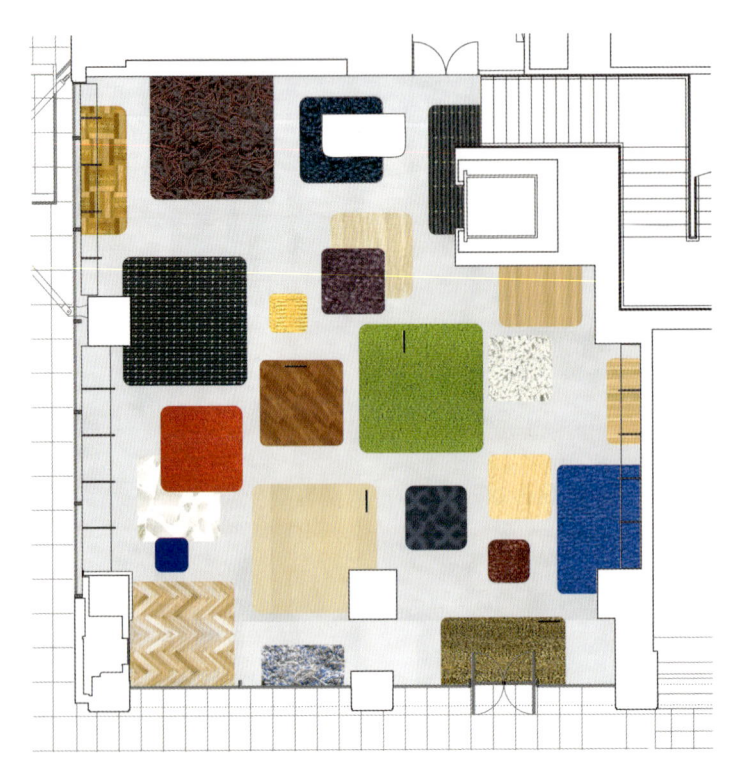

Graphics of the brand concept and commentaries of collaborating designers are located on thin plates oriented at various directions.

向きを変えながら林立する薄いプレートには、ブランドコンセプトや、コラボレーションデザイナーの解説グラフィックが配される。

Like an unfolded fabric sample book, the floor materials and furniture can be rearranged to create an entirely new perspective on the products.

サンプル帳のように広げられた床素材と、そこに置かれる家具を組み替えることで、製品に対する新しい視点を提供する。

HermanMiller Store Tokyo

Curved aluminum frames help to create a varied expression with light, dispelling the sense of homogeneity.
カーブを持ったアルミのフレームは光を受けて表情が変化し、均質さを感じさせない自然な光環境をつくっている。

During seminars, the store's chairs are used to allow customers to test out over a longer period of time. (left)
The storefront exterior facing an avenue in Marunouchi. (right)

セミナー時には商品のチェアを用い、長時間の試座もできる(左)。丸の内の街路に面するストア外観(右)。

THE POWER OF A SINGLE IDEA

SPINNING OBJECTS
回転体 / 2004

The showroom presents many Spinning Objects displaying articles at set heights.

回転体が林立するショールーム。空間全体を一定の高さで抜き取った部分に商品が陳列されている。

A Scenery Populated by Spinning Objects

It is the showroom of a company which deals with hotel furnishings and amenities. They needed to display a huge amount of goods in an effective manner, where in shampoo alone there are at least 10 different types. Furthermore, the company also needed to accommodate new additions without alterations to the structure or causing interference with the design.
We proposed a series of "Spinning Objects", showcases which are like dancers spinning or a potter's wheel. By displaying the items upon the circular cases they become one with the Spinning Objects, populating the space like an after image.
Distorting mirrors along the wall reflect the items, causing them to melt into their surrounding space. Looking at the overall space, the Spinning Objects are expanded by their reflections on the ceiling and the floor, giving this showroom a strong impression.

回転体の林立する風景

宿泊施設の備品やアメニティーを全般的に扱う商社のショールーム。シャンプーつにしても、その種類は何十とあり、それら大量の類似品を効果的に展示し、さらに商品が今後増え続けても、それに耐え得る強さを持った空間を目指した。
そこで、回転しているダンサーやろくろでつくった壺などをモチーフにし、「回転体」と呼ぶ什器のある空間を提案した。什器の円盤上に陳列された多くの商品は、回転体の一部として環状に連続していく。日常的な商品群が、まるで残像のように増殖する。
壁面スリット奥のゆがんだミラーの反射効果により、商品と空間が溶け合う。一方、空間全体を見てみると、床、天井に映り込むことで、上下に引き伸ばされた回転体の林立する風景が、このショールームを強く印象付けることとなる。

THE POWER OF A SINGLE IDEA

The images of the Spinning Objects are expanded by their reflections on the ceiling. (top)
天井面に映り込むことで引き伸ばされる回転体の像（上）。

Identical items are concentrically displayed on the circular cases, creating an illusion like an after image. Spinning Objects in the middle of the air are supported by pillars with a mirror finish. (bottom)
同心円状に並べられる商品がどれも類似していることをポジティブにとらえ、残像のように見せることを提案した。回転体の中段は鏡面仕上げの支柱で浮いているように見せている（下）。

SPINNING OBJECTS

The ribs are made of painted medium-density fiberboard. The primary material is concealed under layers of urethane paint.
リブのディテールは積層したリングによるもの。MDFにウレタン塗装を重ね塗りして、素材感を出さないようにしている。

Stacked rings make up the body of the Spinning Objects.
回転体の製作時の様子。リング状にカットされたパーツを慎重に積み上げていく。ろくろで陶器をつくっているようにも見える。

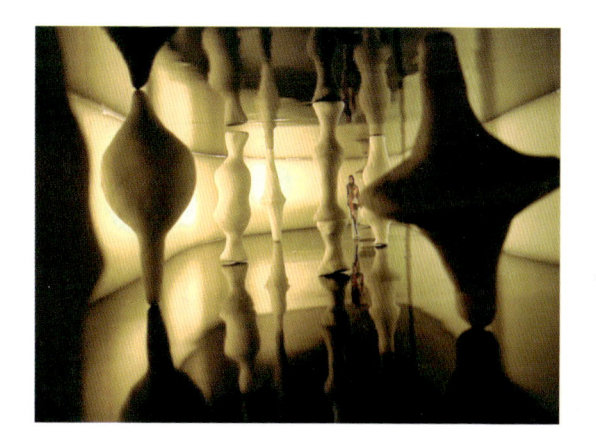

The first mockup model also shows the reflections of the Spinning Objects repeated on the ceiling and the floor.
一番最初のプレゼンテーションで用いた模型。天地に映り込んで増幅する回転体のイメージは、ほぼ最終形と変わらない。

EXHIBITION UNDERGROUND
地下展 UNDERGROUND / 2007

White Space to Experience the Depth of Underground

We created the set for the exhibition "Underground" held at the National Museum of Emerging Science and Innovation in Odaiba. We were required to make visitors physically experience a route that starts at the surface and ends at the core of the earth. We proposed a display where the further visitors walked into the exhibition, the higher the styrene blocks grew around them – a three-dimensional exhibition space that provides the sensation of going ever deeper underground.

The large exhibition hall of 1600m² is composed of 6500 blocks of foamed styrene. The white space, covered with unitary modules of foamed styrene, has a strong appeal and works as a flattering background for the showpieces.

By using this material, we were able to finish setting up the large space within a single week. Furthermore, almost 100% of the material were able to be recycled after the exhibition, thus providing a solution to how exhibitions held at temporary facilities can be dismantled.

地下の深さを体感する白い空間

東京・お台場にある日本科学未来館の企画展「地下展 UNDERGROUND」の会場構成。"地下"についてさまざまな視点から考察する内容で、地表面から始まり、地球の最深部まで至る展示の流れを、体感的に実現することが求められた。

そこで、奥へ進むにつれて段状に周囲が高くなっていくことによって、深く潜っていく感覚になれるような立体的な展示空間を提案した。

1600㎡の会場は、6500個の発泡スチロールブロックの積層によって構成されている。単一モジュールで覆われた白い空間は、圧倒的な迫力を持ち合わせると同時に、展示物を引き立てる背景でもある。

発泡スチロールを用いたことで、気積の大きな空間をわずか1週間ほどで仕上げることが可能となった。また、展示期間終了後、ほぼ100%溶解させて再利用できることで、仮設の展示空間の撤去計画に一つの解答を与えられたと考えている。

EXHIBITION UNDERGROUND

At the very core, visitors explore history on a 4.6 billion year old Earth through an interactive audiovisual installation. (p.72)

展示の"最深部"にあたるゾーン。音と映像を使ったインタラクティブな展示によって46億年の歴史を持つ地球のシステムをダイナミックに感じられる(p.72)。

The planned exhibition was one of the largest in the museum's history. The further visitors walked the higher the styrene blocks piled. These were used as light cases, screens upon which messages are projected or signage on which letters are carved.

日本科学未来館としても、最大規模の企画展示。手前から徐々に高くなっていく発泡スチロールの積層。透かして照明としている部分、映像の投影面、切り文字のサインなど、素材の加工性のよさを利用し、使い方にバリエーションを持たせた。

THE POWER OF A SINGLE IDEA

We used three such kinds of styrene: 40%, 50% and 90%, in foamed blocks (500×500×400mm) of varying softness and lightness.
使用している発泡スチロールブロックは、大きさ (500×500×400mm) こそ同じだが、3種類の発泡率があり、下から上へ向かって、40%、50%、90%と柔らかく、かつ軽いものを使っている。

EXHIBITION UNDERGROUND

A grid was taped onto the floor to ensure precision when layering the blocks. (top)
設営の様子。ブロックの設置する場所を正確にするため、床面をグリッド状にテーピングしている（上）。

The higher blocks are supported by concealed wooden frameworks. (bottom)
展示通路からは見えない裏側。高い位置にあるブロックは木組みで支持される（下）。

THE POWER OF A SINGLE IDEA

HOUSE IN NAKAMARU

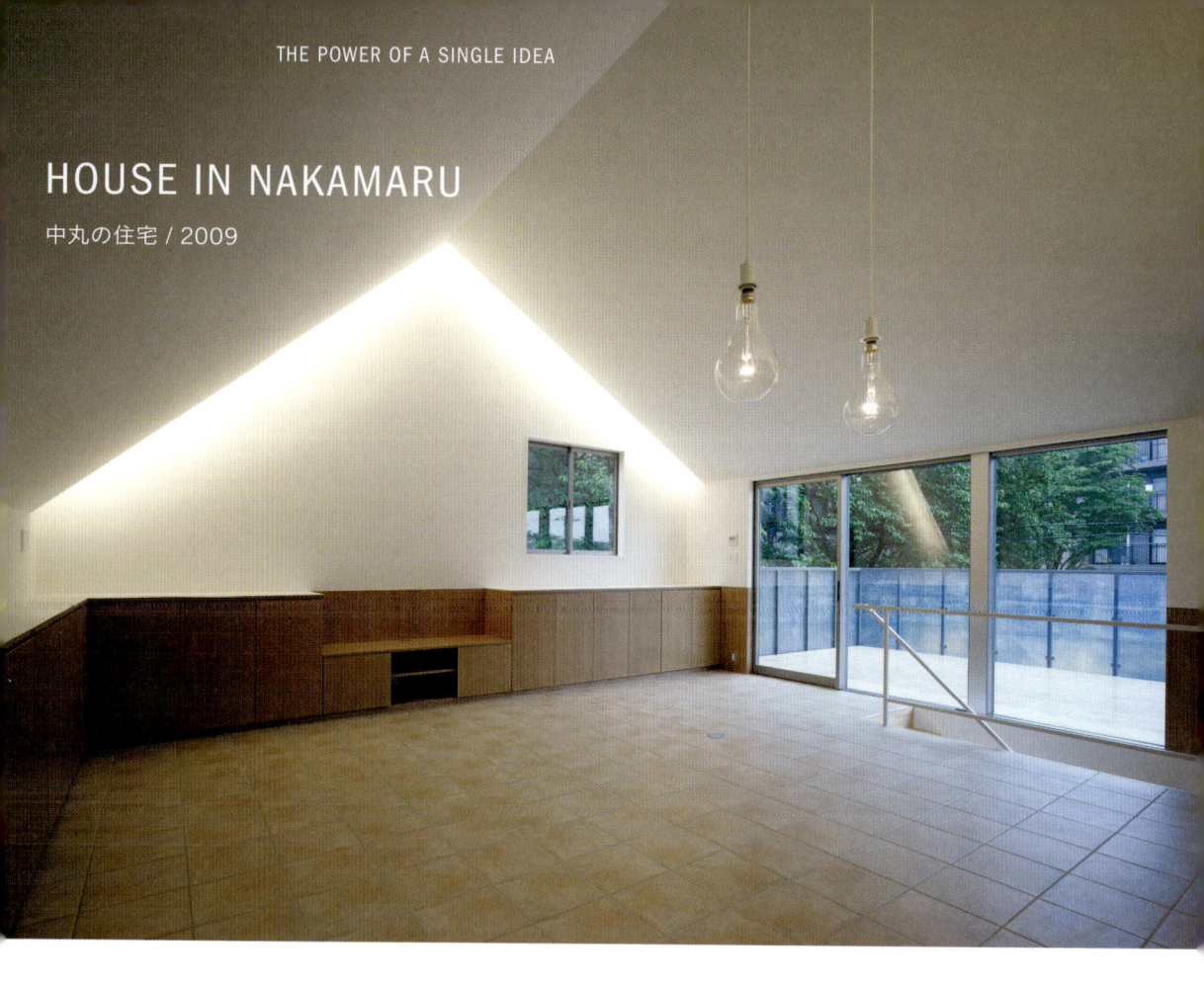

中丸の住宅 / 2009

A Large Terrace Extending from the Living Room

The married couple living in this small house with their pet dog requested for a space where they can enjoy their environment from the comfort of their lofty terrace and tiled floors. The site is located on high ground offering a view of the Port of Yokohama and that of a big cherry blossom tree facing the house in a school ground across the street. Utilitarian rooms such as the master bedroom and bathroom are located on the 1F, while a large single open space serving as a living room can be found on the 2F. The furnishings discretely rise from the tiled floor to merge in with the color and height of the panel walls, gently encircling the lower part of the room. The vessel thus formed under the inclined white ceiling above can hold many pieces of furniture without a hint of disorderliness. The large terrace acts as an open extension of the main floor by using the same tiles as the living room.

リビングを拡張する大きなテラス

夫婦と犬のための小さな住宅。敷地は横浜港を望む高台で、道を挟んで建つ学校には大きな桜の木が植わっている。その立地からも、周辺の環境を楽しむことのできる、開放的で大きなテラスとタイル張りの空間が望まれた。

1階に寝室、水回りなどを配し、2階は大きなワンルームのリビングとなる。床をタイル張りとし、腰壁の高さまで同じ色調の家具が立ち上がり、空間を器のように包み込む。この器に勾配屋根に合わせた白い天井がかぶさる。物が多くなってもその受け皿となって、雑然としないような骨格とした。

大きく張り出したテラスはリビングと同じタイル張りの床が連続し、一体化して開放的な居住空間となる。

The roof-shaped ceiling gently frames the upper floor living room where the tiled floor and low wall act as a vessel.

タイル張りの床と腰壁や家具が空間を器のように受け止め、屋根と同形の天井が柔らかくかぶさる2階のリビング。

HOUSE IN NAKAMARU

The large terrace is covered by a raised canopy, offering maximum light intake.
大きく張り出したテラスと、日差しを最大限採り入れるため、逆勾配となった庇。

The gable roof highlights the residential aspect of the building, contrasting with the adjacent school. The lifted back visor-shaped canopy serves as a gutter to drain rainwater to the back side of the house.
隣接する学校とは対照的に、住居の印象を強めるため、外観は切妻型の形状とした。帽子のつばを跳ね上げたような形状の庇は、雨水を建物奥側の側面まで誘導する雨どいでもある。

Light enters the large terrace doors on the upper floor and reaches the lower level through the staircase.
階段下から2階を見上げる。テラス側の大きな開口から光が落ちてくる。

The structure is exposed in order to give a little more volume to the master bedroom on the 1F.
1階の寝室。天井を少しでも高く感じさせるため、構造体を露出させた。そのことで見えてしまう配線にも表情を持たせた。

77

THE POWER OF A SINGLE IDEA

TORANOANA AKIHABARA
とらのあな AKIHABARA / 2006

Daylight fluorescent lamps, disposed at 600mm intervals, illuminate the whole floor homogeneously white. (left)
600mmごとに配列された昼光色の蛍光灯が店内を白く均質に照らす（左）。

In order to make two kinds of wavy MDF boards look like a single board, we pressed them back-to-back and painted the joints out with urethane. (right)
MDF製の2種類のリブボードの裏面側同士を圧着し、ウレタン塗装で継ぎ目を消して、上下に波形のある、1枚の棚板として見せている（右）。

Merchandise Floating on White Waves

This is an interior design project for a comic store in Akihabara offering music CDs and DVDs. Akihabara, also known as "Electric Town", is the cradle of "moë" culture. Our first aim was to draw out its uniqueness, as well as to emphasize the density and the state of disorderliness of the miscellaneous items.
The display shelves run around the walls like a belt, making the whole floor look like a collector's den. We used ribbed boards to direct our attention to the cut ends of the shelves, which are visible even when the shelves are occupied with plenty of display items. The wave shapes give a unique look and a change to the otherwise monotonous display shelves and emphasize continuity, making the belt of product tiers, together with the belt of waves seem to float in the middle of the white space.

白い波間に浮かぶ商品

秋葉原にあるコミックショップの内装計画。このショップでは音楽CD・DVDソフトを扱う。電気街や"萌え文化"発祥の地として知られる秋葉原。ここでは物の密度の高さや雑多な状態をより強調するような商品の見せ方と、売り場の個性を同時に達成することを第一に考えた。
エントランスから、ショップを一巡する帯のような陳列棚をつくることで、マニアックなコレクターの自室のように、大量のソフトで囲われた空間を目指した。そこで、多くの商品に埋もれても見えてくる部分である棚の小口に注目し、リブボードという凹凸の付いた化粧材の、波形の断面形状を見せる使い方をした。単調になりがちな棚に表情と変化を与え、その連続性を強調する。何層もの商品の帯と、それを構成する波形の帯とが真っ白い空間の中に浮遊する。

EGG ZABUTON

エッグ座布団 / 2006

Sitting on it makes it look like the eggs are being hatched. An experience as unique as it looks, the material also has an excellent pressure distribution effect. (left)

上に座ると、その姿はまるで鶏が卵を温めているかのように見える。素材には優れた体圧分散効果がある (左)。

The wall looks like one big egg pack from which the Egg Zabutons fell out, and the yellow floor makes it looks as if the eggs yolks have been spilt all over. (right)

大きな卵パックが開いたような壁面と、卵の黄身がこぼれたような黄色の床 (右)。

The Loveliness and Strength of Eggs

For the exhibition "Food and Modern Art - Part 2" held at BankART in Yokohama, we contrived the "Egg Zabuton", which was inspired by Arne Jacobsen's masterpiece "Egg Chair", and after considering that a "zabuton" (flat cushion used the floor) would be better suited than a chair in the Japanese way of life.
Each Egg Zabuton is composed of 49 "eggs" (7×7) and its high density and low-repulsion polyurethane foam reduces pressure on the hips.
For the exhibition, we placed 300 paper egg packs on the wall around the Egg Zabutons to make it look as if the eggs had fallen out from the gigantic pack.

卵の愛らしさと強さ

横浜のBankARTで行われた展覧会「食と現代美術part2―美食同源」に出品作家として参加した。エッグチェアというアルネ・ヤコブセンによる名作イスがあるが、日本の生活スタイルに合わせて「エッグ座布団」なるものを考えた。
7個×7個＝49個の"卵"をつなげた座布団で、高密度低反発ウレタンフォーム素材を使用して、おしりや腰にかかる負担を軽減する機能を持つ。
300個の卵の紙パックを会場の壁面に取り付け、たくさんのエッグ座布団がそこからこぼれ落ちてきているような構成とした。

COLUMN 01

THE SOURCE OF TORAFU'S IDEAS

トラフのアイデアソース

Rationality supported by pleasant visuals and logic...
Ideas that are at once familiar and brilliantly cutting-edge... Fantasy and reality.
At first glance, Torafu's works may seem to possess elements that contradict each other but in fact, they coexist quite naturally. What is the source of this style and conception?

楽しさにあふれるビジュアルとロジックに裏付けられた合理性——。
人を受け入れる親しみやすさと切れ味の鮮やかなアイデア——。ファンタジーとリアリティー。
トラフの作品には、一見相反するような要素が実にごく自然に共存している。
こうした仕事の流儀、発想の源はどういったところから生まれるのか。

Recognizing the issues and requirements of a project

Intriguing ideas are what create a large part of the appeal in your work. How do you arrive at your conceptions?

Shinya Kamuro (referred to below as K) My conceptions are sometimes the result of discovering something as I'm walking through town every day. I have an interest in things that generally exist around us but that we tend to overlook. Reflecting on the origins of such things can be really interesting. Physically small things with a subtle presence exert something of an influence on people's behavior and emotions. I think I often use such things to arrive at a conception.

Koichi Suzuno (referred to below as S) Even a single line drawn on the floor can change people's awareness and naturally provoke certain effects. It is often more than enough to simply create this kind of trigger.
I find that theme parks and amusement parks are too one-dimensional because enjoyment is created and focused on all the many choreographed productions. In contrast, locations like snowy mountains and beaches are ideal because they allow us to do so many things and offer such a variety of activities all in one place. I would like to create things according to this way of thinking.
In order to accomplish that for a project, I first try to draw out everything I can from the pre-existing conditions there. I would build a large model of the site to examine the circumstances and environment while communicating carefully with the client as much as possible, in order to discover conditions and settings that may be concealed. By doing so, I will most definitely gain some kind of hint that will lead to new opportunities.

K So I think that we basically won't start a design that is based solely on an idea. That seems to be the methodological way of doing things, but we make a conscious effort to do

プロジェクトの問題や条件に気付く

——二人の仕事は、アイデアの面白さが大きな魅力の一つとなっています。どんなことから発想を得ているのでしょう。

禿 真哉（以下K） 普段街を歩いていて、発見したことから着想することがあります。まわりに普通に存在しているんだけど、見すごされているような要素に興味を持っていて、その成り立ちを考えていくと結構、面白いんです。
物理的には小さい、希薄な存在のものが、人のちょっとした行動や感情に影響を及ぼしている。そういうものを使って何かを考える、ということはすごくあるなと思います。

鈴野浩一（以下S） 床にライン一本引いてあるだけでも人の意識は変わるんですよね。それに誘発されたり、自然に作用が働いたりする。ちょっとしたきっかけをつくってあげるだけでよかったりするわけです。
テーマパークや遊園地のようなたくさんの演出でつくられた楽しさは、一方的に過ぎる気がしています。例えば雪山とか海のように一つの場所でも、いろんな行動を許容する、アクティビティーにも多様性のある状況がいい。そういうものをつくれればと思っています。
実際のプロジェクトでは、そこにある条件をできる限りたくさん引き出していくようにします。大きな敷地模型をつくって状況や環境を検討したり、なるべくクライアントと密にコミュニケーションをとったりして、隠れている固有の条件や設定を見つけていくんです。そうすれば、きっかけを生む手掛かりが必ず出てきます。

K だからアイデアありきで設計を始めるというのは、僕らは基本的にはないと思います。それは、何か方法論的なやり方に終始してしまっているようで、そうではないやり方を意識して取り組むようにしています。

things differently.
Actually, I found methodology interesting when I was a student and used to actively participate in independent seminars and competitions with colleagues. At the time, I must have found some appeal in the pursuit of a strong logic that could be applied under any and all conditions.
However, I soon realized that there was more to it when I actually started to work as an architect. It still goes without saying that solutions are based on existing conditions. I now think that there is more significance in creating something unique based on existing conditions.

S   Speaking of school days, I was more or less the cynical type of student who didn't get absorbed in school subjects. I held doubts concerning the criterion of given subjects and felt that those things were disconnected from reality. I may feel this more strongly since I'm currently in a teaching position at university, but I think that we should progress from setting up conditions by asking "What is required here?"
I really didn't feel any interest in competing over small differences in architectural design. Since I wanted to make propositions from the program itself, I took an interest in urban planning. But rather than building from something big, I now think that the effective placement of one object can have an effect on a town and even society. In that sense, you could say that I first keenly felt the appeal of architecture once I started to deal with real problems on the job. I think that one way of creating things is by breaking down the things we take for granted and seeing them afresh through a reverse process.

Creating various things from architecture

You are not only fixated on architecture but also actively involved in interior and product work.

K   After graduating from university and getting practical work experience as an architect, I felt as though this was not an age where architects could create buildings just like sculptures or that architecture could resolve anything by itself. From the viewpoint of design, I discovered many things as I watched the work of others involved. For example, I was reminded that there are other things that are as socially valued as architecture without relying simply on solid modeling and principles alone.
It was probably this kind of broadened outlook that led me to start accepting work other than architecture.

S   We can also build products and furniture based on archi-

確かに、僕は学生の時に仲間と自主的な研究会やコンペなどを活発にやっていて、そのときは方法論みたいなものを面白がっているところがありました。当時は（条件に対して）どこでも通用する強度を持ったロジックの追求に魅力を感じていたのでしょう。
ところが、実際の建築の仕事をするうちにそれだけではないことに気付き始めました。ある条件があって、何かを解決するということには変わらないんですけどね。そこにしか生まれ得ないことをつくる方が意味がある、と思い直したんです。

S　学生の時といえば、僕はどちらかというと斜に構えているタイプで、学校の課題もそこまで夢中になれなかった。与えられた課題の条件自体に対して疑問を持ったりして、リアリティーを感じられなかったんですね。今は大学で教える立場でもあるから、余計に感じますが、「そこに何が必要か」というような条件設定からやらないといけないと思うんです。
だから、建築デザインのちょっとした差異を競っていても全然面白くない、と感じていました。プログラムそのものから提案をしたいと思っていたので、都市計画にも興味がありましたが、今は大きなところからつくるよりも、一つ何かを置くことで街や社会にも影響を与えられるのではないか、と考えています。そういう意味で、僕は実務でリアルな問題に触れるようになって、初めて建築の面白さが感じられるようになりました。
当たり前のようにあるものでも、一旦解体して見つめ直す。そういう逆のプロセスをたどることも、クリエーションの一つの手段だと思っています。

建築からさまざまなものを生み出す

―― 建築だけにこだわらず、インテリアやプロダクトの仕事も積極的にされています。

K　（大学を卒業して）僕は実務をやりながら、建築家が彫刻のように建物をつくることのできる時代ではないんだろうな、と感じていました。あるいは建築一つだけで何かが解決できるようなことでもなくなってきたと。
実際に設計をする視点でいろいろな人の仕事を見ていくと、多くの発見がありました。例えば、強い造形や理念だけを支えにしていくことなく、社会的にも建築としても評価され得るものがあることにも改めて気付きました。
そうして視野が広がったことが、建築以外の仕事も受け入れる起点になっているかもしれません。

COLUMN 01

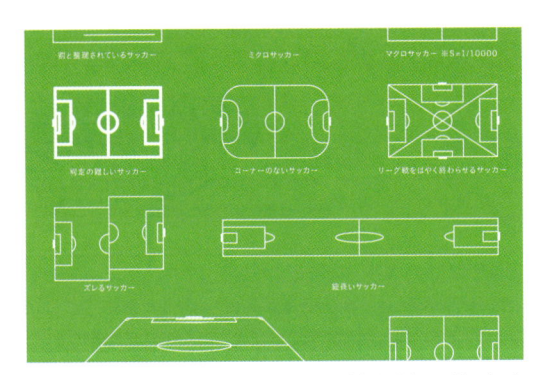

This project expands the possibilities of the game of football (soccer) by simply playing with the white lines on the pitch (field of play).
ピッチの白線を変えるだけでサッカーの可能性を広げるプロジェクト

A taxi stand made with painted lines only.
ラインだけでつくられたタクシーの待機スペース

A bench secured to the wall by its backrest only.
背板だけが壁に固定されたベンチ

Roofing made of slates that resemble pieces of confectionery.
お菓子のような屋根のスレート材

An area divided by a single leveling string.
水糸1本だけで領域を分ける

Callers can look as though they are getting a perm.
電話している人がパーマをかけられているように見える

Packaged cut-out characters made of stainless steel before assembly.
梱包された施工前のステンレスの切り文字

THE SOURCE OF TORAFU'S IDEAS

COLUMN 01

A section view of a piece of playground equipment in a park.
断面が見える公園の遊具

A project to build a viewing platform in a position that balances gravity and centrifugal force.
重力と遠心力のつり合う位置に「展望台」をつくるプロジェクト

A standing figure carved in brick.
レンガで彫刻された立像

Shading that gives the appearance of water drops.
影が水玉の模様をつくる

Concrete stairs that can look very thin depending on the angle.
角度によって薄っぺらく見えるコンクリートの階段

Coins swirling into a collection box.
コインが円を描いて転がっていく募金箱

Mail boxes picketed at a distance from their houses in Australia.
家から離れて並んでいるオーストラリアの郵便箱

COLUMN 01

tectural methods and procedures. I think that the architectural perspective we possess really is a great asset.
We envisage a site by imagining the kind of situation in which the furniture and products would be used. This helps us to draw out the conditions.
K   I do product and interior work following the same kind of steps as I would with that kind of architectural design. I also keep doing architecture, of course. It's hard to put into words, but I feel that this makes a difference. This kind of diversity is what I believe creates the characteristics of Torafu.
S   With architecture, you can find a really broad range of specialists involved depending on the scope of the project. The ability to produce various collaborations comes naturally to architects, and I think that architecture is all about designing the circumstances. Creating things in many different genres has led to an increase in that kind of involvement.

Broadening the scope

It is now eight years since you went independent and established Torafu. Your work is steadily expanding.

S   Right now we are really blessed with clients and are getting requests from people who respond to our work. I think that, despite being an architectural design company, the fact that we can design shop interiors and products helps to explain this situation. I hope that we can broaden our scope as an extension of that, and design everything from architecture to furniture and products from start to finish. I'm not that conscious of the genre itself, but I do really enjoy working with an architectural approach.
K   Regardless of the type of project, there is never just one correct solution. Instead, another way of doing things is by slightly shifting the solution so that you can arrive at a different way of seeing things. This is something I learned after having graduated from school and I still feel its influence now. There is nothing interesting about ideas that are forced upon you. On the contrary, one of the important things for us is to leave enough room for others to be able to participate in the design. This method also works well in meetings with clients. Since design involves a communicative aspect, I think it is necessary to be receptive and communicate with many different people.
That is exactly why we would like to design the context of that situation rather than just one object or building. We want to approach the entire thing as a kind of landscape.

S　建築の考え方や進め方をベースに、プロダクトや家具をつくることもできます。僕らは建築的な視点でものをとらえられることが武器になるんじゃないかって思っています。
家具もプロダクトも使われるシチュエーションを想像して、"敷地"を想定しています。それが条件を引き出す手掛かりになるんです。
K　そうした建築の設計と同じようなステップを踏んで、プロダクトやインテリアの仕事をしていく。そしてもちろん、建築もちゃんとつくっていく。そうすることで、言葉ではっきりとは言えないかもしれないのですが、違うところはあるだろうなと思っています。いろいろやることで（トラフとしての）特徴のようなものが生まれているかもしれない、と感じています。
S　建築ならその規模に応じてプロジェクトに関わる専門家も多岐に渡りますよね。さまざまなコラボレーションを生み出すプロデュース能力は建築家ならではのものだし、そういうことも含めて建築は状況を設計していくということかな、と思っています。いろいろなジャンルのものをつくることでそうした関わりも増えています。

豊かさを広げる

──トラフとして独立して、8年目になりました。二人の仕事はどんどん広がっています。

S　今は、本当にクライアントに恵まれていて、僕らの仕事に共感した人たちが頼んでくれています。建築設計事務所なのにショップのインテリアやプロダクトのデザインができるのは、それを裏付けているのかなとも思います。その延長でもっと範囲を広げて、建築から家具、プロダクトもトータルでデザインできるようになれば面白いな、と期待もしています。
ジャンル自体はそこまで強く意識しているわけではないですが、建築的なアプローチで取り組めることを楽しんでいます。
K　どんなプロジェクトでも正解が決まっているわけではありません。むしろ答えをあえて少しだけずらすことで、違う見え方ができてくる、そういうやり方もある。やはり学校を出てから覚えたことですが、今もその影響があるかなと。
考えを押し付けられても面白くないですし、逆にデザインの中に他の人が入り込めるような余地をつくっておくというのは、僕らにとって大事なことですね。クライアントとの打ち合わせでもそういう方がうまくいきますし、デザインはコミュニケーションの面を持っているから、いろいろな人とのやり取りが生まれるよう

S Sometimes I think that it's not necessary to build anything new in this age of overabundance. I think that, in this kind of age, we should become more conscious of our stance in regard to the process of creation. In fact, my conception starts from the point of asking "Wouldn't it be better not to build anything?"
So rather than spending money and resources to build something exaggerated, you can create new sensations by simply altering a perspective or cutting something off.
Let's take for example the "airvase" (p.180), it has no strict functionality so anyone can come up with a way to use it, as its color and shape are subject to the eye of the beholder. The image of paper is overturned and its potentials expanded at once. In that regard, I feel that it symbolizes our stance. Architecture isn't something that you can take in your hands and show around, but this product is now being sold in cities around the globe and we are surprised by the rate at which this expansion is taking place. We are overjoyed when we think about how our way of thinking is prevailing with it.

な、多様な受け皿を持たせることが必要なんだと思います。
だからこそ、僕らは一つの物や建築というよりは、その背景となる状況をデザインしたい。全体を風景として提案していきたいなと考えています。
S これだけ物があふれている時代に、僕らがわざわざ何かを新しくつくる必要はないのではないかって考えてしまう。それよりもそういう時代においては、物をつくるスタンスというものに意識的になるべきだと思います。むしろ、つくらなくていいんじゃないか、というところから発想していかないといけない。
いろいろなコストや資源を費やして大げさなものをつくらなくても、視点や切り取り方を変えてみるだけで、豊かに感じられることがたくさんあります。
例えば、「空気の器」(p.180)は、機能が強くあるわけでもないですが、人によっていろいろな使い方ができるし、色やカタチもさまざまな見え方をする。あるいは紙に対する印象が覆り、その可能性が一気に広がっていく。そういう意味で僕らのスタンスを象徴してくれている気もします。
建築は持っていって見せられないけれど、これはすでに世界中の都市で販売されていて、その広がりの早さに驚いています。僕らの考え方が、少しずつ広がっていく、そう思うととてもうれしく感じます。

TORAFU ARCHITECTS IDEA + PROCESS 2004-2011

PROFILE
プロフィール

Illustration by Yuichi Yokoyama
イラスト：横山裕一

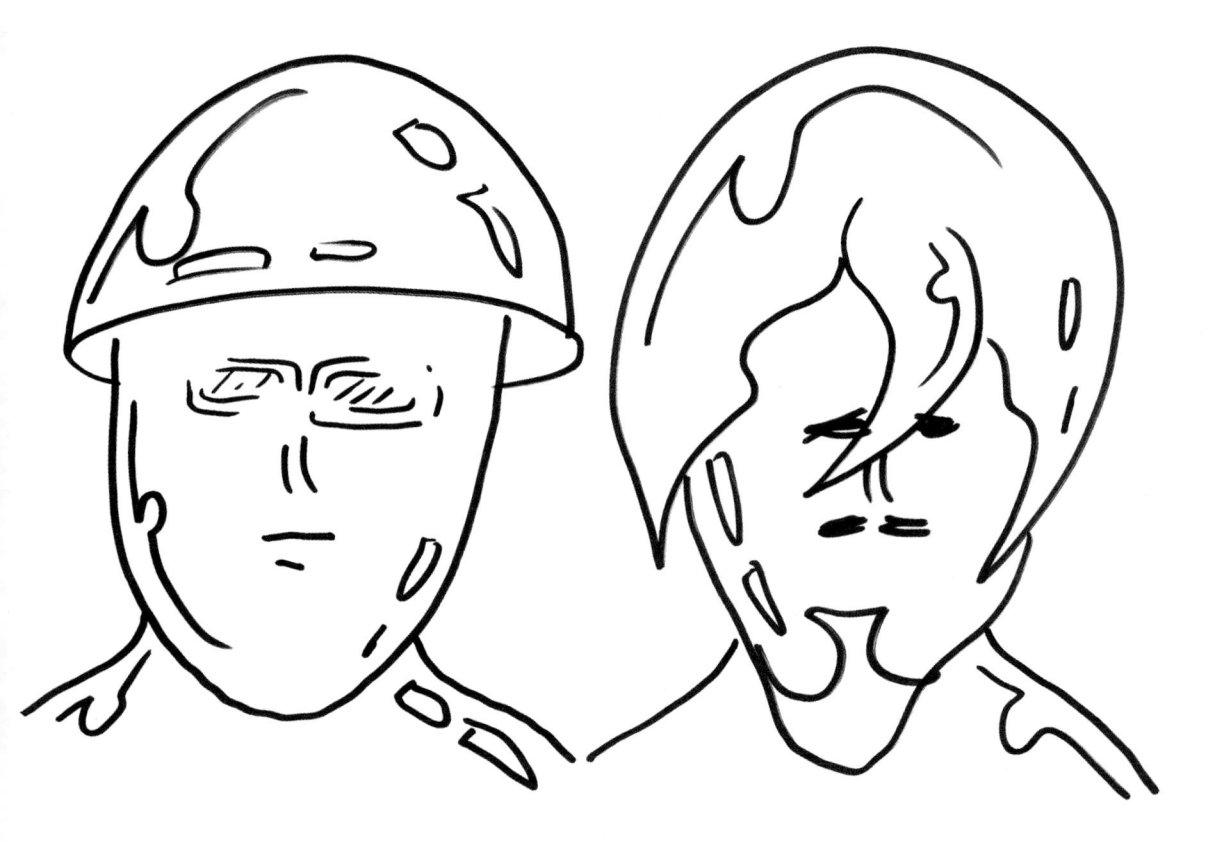

Koichi Suzuno
鈴野浩一

1973: Born in Kanagawa Prefecture
1996: Graduated from Department of Architecture, Tokyo University of Science
1998: Completed the Master Course of Architecture, Yokohama National University
1998-2001: Worked at Coelacanth K&H
2002-2003: Worked at Kerstin Thompson Architects / Melbourne
2004-: Established TORAFU ARCHITECTS with Shinya Kamuro
2005-2008: Lecturer at Tokyo University of Science
2008-: Lecturer at Showa Women's University
2010-: Lecturer at Musashino Art University and Kyoritsu Women's University

1973年　神奈川県生まれ
1996年　東京理科大学工学部建築学科卒業
1998年　横浜国立大学大学院工学部建築学専攻修士課程修了
1998〜2001年　シーラカンス K&H 勤務
2002〜2003年　Kerstin Thompson Architects(メルボルン) 勤務
2004年〜　トラフ建築設計事務所 共同主宰
2005〜2008年　東京理科大学非常勤講師
2008年〜　昭和女子大学非常勤講師
2010年〜　武蔵野美術大学、共立女子大学非常勤講師

Shinya Kamuro
禿 真哉

1974: Born in Shimane Prefecture
1997: Graduated from Department of Architecture, School of Science & Technology, Meiji University
1999: Completed the Master Course of Architecture, Meiji University
2000-2003: Worked at Jun Aoki & Associates
2004-: Established TORAFU ARCHITECTS with Koichi Suzuno
2008-: Lecturer at Showa Women's University

1974年　島根県生まれ
1997年　明治大学理工学部建築学科卒業
1999年　同大学大学院修士課程修了
2000〜2003年　青木淳建築計画事務所勤務
2004年〜　トラフ建築設計事務所 共同主宰
2008年〜　昭和女子大学非常勤講師

3

MATERIALS AND GRAPHICS
素材とグラフィック

Building a space starting from
a single material or graphical motif.
一つの素材やグラフィックをきっかけに
空間をつくっていく。

MATERIALS AND GRAPHICS

NEW PEOPLE
NEW PEOPLE / 2009

NEW PEOPLE

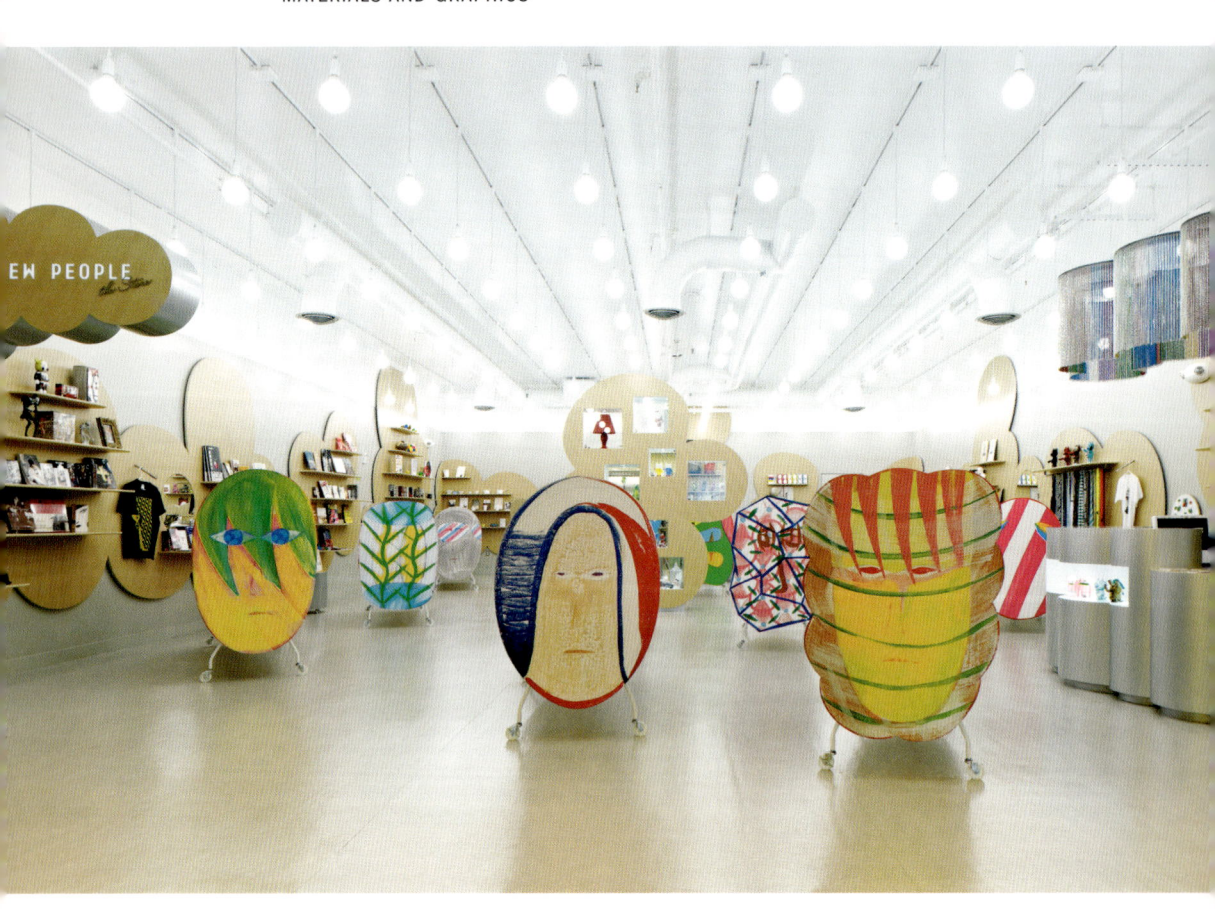

A Space between 2D and 3D

The "NEW PEOPLE" J-Pop Culture complex opened in the heart of Japan Town, San Francisco, which aims to become a center showcasing modern Japanese popular culture. We were primarily involved with designing the interior of the public spaces such as the lobby on the 1F, the "NEW PEOPLE the Store" retail shop on the mezzanine, as well as a gallery and offices located on the 3F. The building also houses a movie theater in the basement and various tenants on the 2F.
The side panels of the displays in the mezzanine shop feature the faces of characters which appear in manga by Yuichi Yokoyama, bringing out qualities of the 2D medium into real space. The "Face Furniture" characters seem to engage in a lively dialogue with each other through the speech bubble-shaped displays on the floor and walls. By mixing manga as a motif into real spaces, we produced an abstract yet intriguing effect that brings out the best from the 2D and 3D worlds. Furthermore, we were inspired by the building's name to create a space where one can live a unique and surrealistic experience and foster the appreciation of modern Japanese popular culture by all visitors to NEW PEOPLE.

二次元と三次元の間

サンフランシスコのジャパンタウンにオープンした、日本のポップカルチャーをテーマにした複合施設「NEW PEOPLE」。地下1階にはシアター、中2階にはショップ「NEW PEOPLE the Store」、2階にテナント、3階がギャラリーとオフィスという構成になっている。そのうち、ロビーなどの共有スペース、ショップ、ギャラリー、オフィスの内装を手掛けた。
中2階のショップは、漫画の持つ二次元で薄っぺらな感じを活かしたいと考えた。アーティストの横山裕一の漫画に登場するキャラクターの顔を側面に転写し、「顔什器」と呼ぶディスプレイによる空間を提案した。壁面ディスプレイや平置き什器の形状も、漫画の吹き出しをモチーフにし、ショップに現れたキャラクターが会話しているような賑わいを持たせた。漫画というモチーフと現実空間の融合によって、二次元と三次元の間を標榜するような不思議な抽象性を生む。この"白々しさ"とも言える独特な雰囲気での体験を通じて、NEW PEOPLEという名前通りに、訪れた人が日本の新しいカルチャーに共鳴できるような空間を目指した。

By taking a step aside, the faces on the displays vanish into 2D space, revealing the products showcased. (top and bottom)
顔什器の横に立つと、二次元の薄っぺらな顔は消え、陳列された商品が際立って見えてくる（上・下）。

The NEW PEOPLE the Store retail shop on the mezzanine showcase mobile displays imprinted with manga characters by artist Yuichi Yokoyama. (p.90)
中２階のショップNEW PEOPLE the Store。横山裕一による漫画のキャラクターの顔が転写された可動式のディスプレイ什器が立ち並ぶ (p.90)。

MATERIALS AND GRAPHICS

NEW PEOPLE is located in San Francisco's Japan Town and is managed by VIZ Pictures – a Japanese cinema distributor in the USA.

サンフランシスコのジャパンタウンにあるNEW PEOPLE。日本映画をアメリカで配給するビズピクチャーズが運営している。

The five-storied pagoda offers an exotic sight from the offices. (middle)
The gallery on the 3F. (bottom left)

五重塔がそびえるエキゾチックな風景が望めるオフィス（中）。
3階のギャラリー（左下）。

The wall inside the entrance lobby. Floor signage and short messages are written on the acrylic panels.

入口ロビーの壁面。フロアサインのほかに、短いメッセージが書かれたアクリルパネルが並んでいる。

MATERIALS AND GRAPHICS

Exhibition of minä perhonen
ミナ ペルホネンのエキシビション / 2007–2009

minä perhonen's third installation "Rainwear In / Rainwear Out" (2009). The house-shaped booth highlights the "inside" and "outside" with walls prominently featuring the brand's "sunny rain" textile pattern.

3回目となる2009年の展示会のテーマは「雨のウチ・ソト」。ブースを家型とすることで、"ウチ"と"ソト"を強く印象付ける計画とした。壁面はミナ ペルホネンの「sunny rain」というテキスタイルのパターンを大きく引き伸ばした。

Chairs shaped like rain drops make for a fun day in the rain.
雨粒をモチーフにしたイスも楽しい"雨の日"を演出する。

Exhibition of minä perhonen

The first installation "Lifestyle of minä perhonen" (2007). The circular booth allows customers to approach it from any angle and appreciate the fashion brand's exclusive fabric pattern called "forest parade" which was applied on its outer surface.

2007年の最初の展示「ライフスタイル オブ ミナ ペルホネン」。どの方向からも正面となる利点を活かしつつ、人が円滑に移動できるよう円形のブースとした。壁面は、ミナ ペルホネンの「forest parade」というテキスタイルのパターンをまとっている。

The second installation "minä perhonen and Life Design" (2008). A fish scale motif named "mermaid" adorns the circular booth, and is echoed by the shape of the openings.

2回目の2008年の展示「ミナ ペルホネンと生活デザイン」。円形ブースに大きく引き伸ばした「mermaid」といううろこ模様のテキスタイルのパターンを張り、この模様に合わせて開口部の形を切り抜いた。

Like a Travelling Circus

"The Stage" is an exhibition space located at the center of Isetan department store's 1F in Shinjuku. The platform can be accessed from all directions, offering great visibility to the various one week events held there by designer brands such as minä perhonen.
A temporary exhibition that is expected to be held every following year, we had envisioned the image of a circus travelling from town to town that eventually returns to the same marquee.

巡回するサーカスのように

伊勢丹 新宿店本館の1階中央にある催事スペース「ザ・ステージ」。1週間単位でさまざまなイベントが行われ、周囲が通路になっているため、全方位から見られる注目度の高い場所である。
この場所で、ミナ ペルホネンが期間限定の展示を開催した。次の年にもこの場所で展示することを想定し、さながら各地を巡回するサーカスのような印象を持たせる提案とした。

MATERIALS AND GRAPHICS

3M store

3M ストア / 2010

A brand store with a limited opening period, it faces Omotesando Hills and serves as a kind of showcase with the white framing.

表参道ヒルズ向かいに位置する期間限定のストア。白いフレーミングによって、ショーケースのような役割を果たしている。

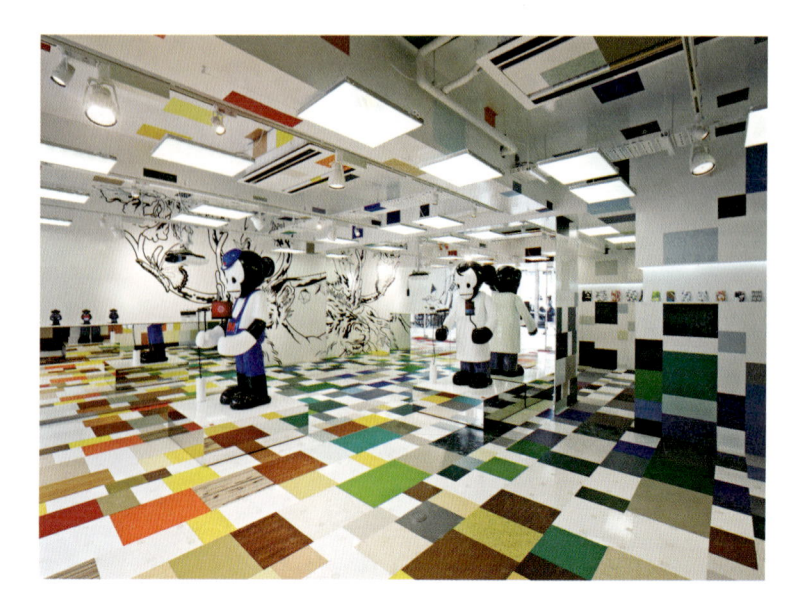

The 1F is a showroom and also a custom order corner for 3M DI-NOC sheets, which have been utilized graphically.

1階はショールームとシートのカスタムオーダーのコーナーからなる。3Mのダイノックシートをグラフィカルに使用した。

3M store

The 2F features a display of 3M products on column-shaped racks that resemble trees in the midst of a forest.
2階には円柱形のラックを森の中の木々のように配置し、3Mの商品を陳列。

Where Materials and Products Themselves Give Form to the Space

素材や商品そのものが形づくる空間

The maker of Post-it Notes, DI-NOC Film sheets and chemical products, 3M, opened its first concept store for a limited period of time.
The interior of the 3M store feels like a walk-in catalog almost entirely made using 3M materials and goods to further promote awareness of the brand's product line-up, which is known for its variety and technical innovations.
The 1F features an "Exhibition Area" showcasing practical applications of 3M products and a custom order corner called the "Meister Area". Customers can walk into the store on a tile floor inspired by the street's distinctive pavement pattern, before it gradually turns into a multicolored surface as they move to the back of the store. The checkered pattern then scatters onto the columns and walls, making its way up to the ceiling.
The 2F offers a massive selection of 3M products for sale on circular display shelves. All items in stock are put forward in this fashion at once to convey the variety and quantity of products made by 3M. Well garnished layers of colorful packages dress up the core of these tree-like structures. Contrasting against the white background, 3M's colorful products appear floating in the white space.

ポストイットやダイノックシートで知られる化学素材メーカー、3M初の期間限定コンセプトストア。
豊富な商品カテゴリーと独自技術を持つ3Mの製品が一般にも広く認知されるよう、店内の仕上げにはほぼすべてにわたって同社の製品や素材を使い、まるでサンプル帳のような店舗を目指した。
1階は、製品技術のショールームとカスタムオーダーのコーナーからなる。歩道のタイルパターンがそのまま店内に伸びており、奥へ向かって徐々に色を変化させる。柱や壁面がそのパターンを吸い上げるようにして、密度を減らしながら天井へと展開している。
2階は、3Mの製品を大量に陳列した売り場となっている。ストックも表に見せることで商品の点数や物量をアピールできると考え、円柱形の什器を木々のように点在させた。商品を環状に積層して陳列し、3Mの素材や商品そのものが白い空間に彩りを与え、浮かび上がって見えてくる。

MATERIALS AND GRAPHICS

yozakura (Kaneka Milano Salone 2011)
yozakura (Kaneka Milano Salone 2011) / 2011

yozakura (Kaneka Milano Salone 2011)

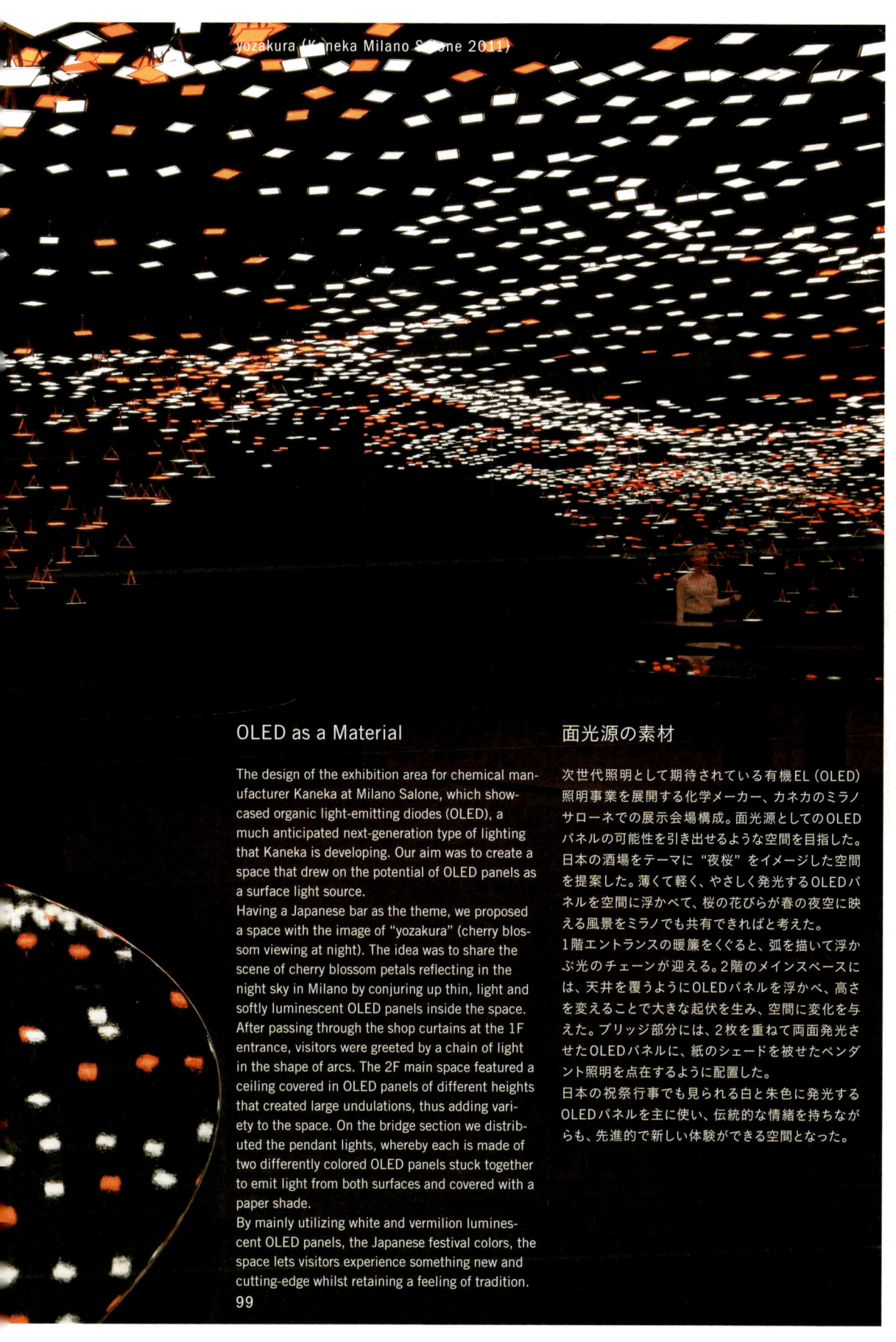

OLED as a Material

The design of the exhibition area for chemical manufacturer Kaneka at Milano Salone, which showcased organic light-emitting diodes (OLED), a much anticipated next-generation type of lighting that Kaneka is developing. Our aim was to create a space that drew on the potential of OLED panels as a surface light source.
Having a Japanese bar as the theme, we proposed a space with the image of "yozakura" (cherry blossom viewing at night). The idea was to share the scene of cherry blossom petals reflecting in the night sky in Milano by conjuring up thin, light and softly luminescent OLED panels inside the space. After passing through the shop curtains at the 1F entrance, visitors were greeted by a chain of light in the shape of arcs. The 2F main space featured a ceiling covered in OLED panels of different heights that created large undulations, thus adding variety to the space. On the bridge section we distributed the pendant lights, whereby each is made of two differently colored OLED panels stuck together to emit light from both surfaces and covered with a paper shade.
By mainly utilizing white and vermilion luminescent OLED panels, the Japanese festival colors, the space lets visitors experience something new and cutting-edge whilst retaining a feeling of tradition.

面光源の素材

次世代照明として期待されている有機EL（OLED）照明事業を展開する化学メーカー、カネカのミラノサローネでの展示会場構成。面光源としてのOLEDパネルの可能性を引き出せるような空間を目指した。日本の酒場をテーマに"夜桜"をイメージした空間を提案した。薄くて軽く、やさしく発光するOLEDパネルを空間に浮かべて、桜の花びらが春の夜空に映える風景をミラノでも共有できればと考えた。
1階エントランスの暖簾をくぐると、弧を描いて浮かぶ光のチェーンが迎える。2階のメインスペースには、天井を覆うようにOLEDパネルを浮かべ、高さを変えることで大きな起伏を生み、空間に変化を与えた。ブリッジ部分には、2枚を重ねて両面発光させたOLEDパネルに、紙のシェードを被せたペンダント照明を点在するように配置した。
日本の祝祭行事でも見られる白と朱色に発光するOLEDパネルを主に使い、伝統的な情緒を持ちながらも、先進的で新しい体験ができる空間となった。

MATERIALS AND GRAPHICS

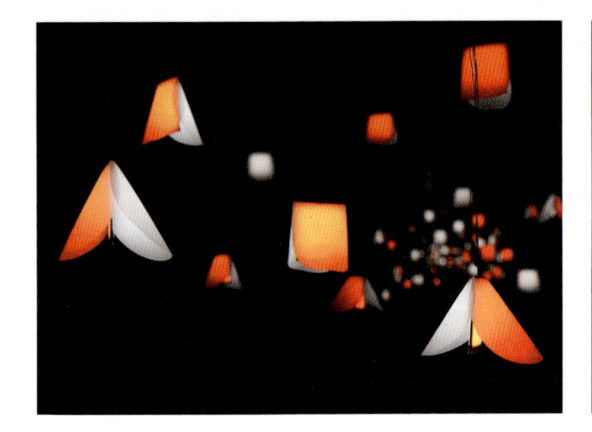

Pendant lights displayed on the bridge section of the site's top floor. OLED panels of two different colors were used to illuminate the two sides of each paper shade.

会場最上階のブリッジ部には、ペンダント照明を展示。2枚の色の違うOLEDパネルを使って両面に発光させ、それに紙のシェードを被せている。

The reception area with a Japanese style shop curtain. The art work was produced by the design unit "wabisabi".

暖簾が掛けられた受付。アートワークはデザインユニット「ワビサビ」によるもの。

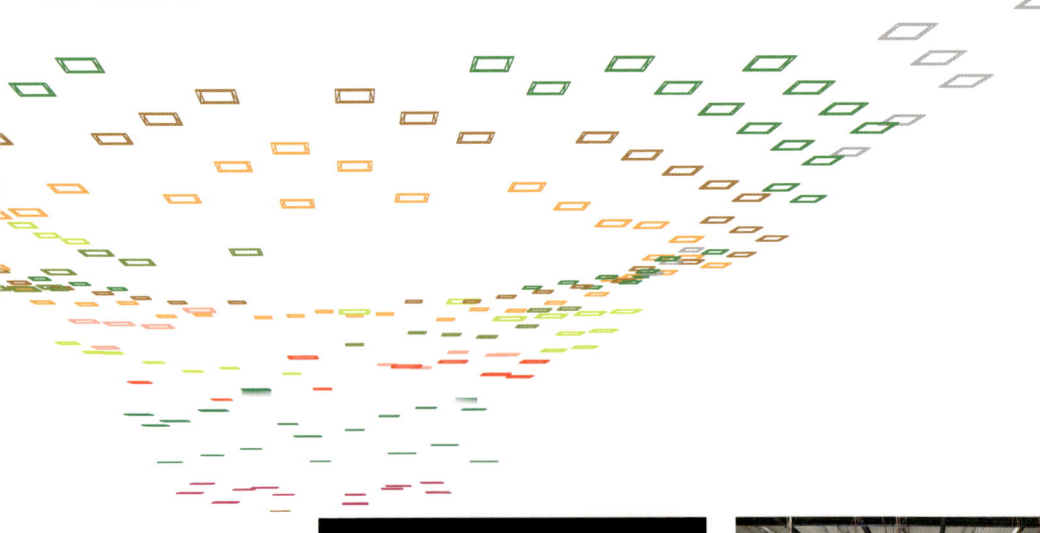

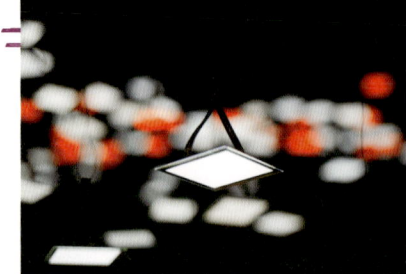

A thin, light OLED panel hanging from the ceiling.

天井から吊り下げられた、むきだしの薄くて軽いOLEDパネル。

Each of the approximately 2500 OLED panels were wired and hung from the ceiling after deciding the appropriate height and position.

約2500枚におよぶOLEDパネルの一枚一枚に配線をし、高さや位置をすべて決めて天井から吊っている。

yozakura (Kaneka Milano Salone 2011)

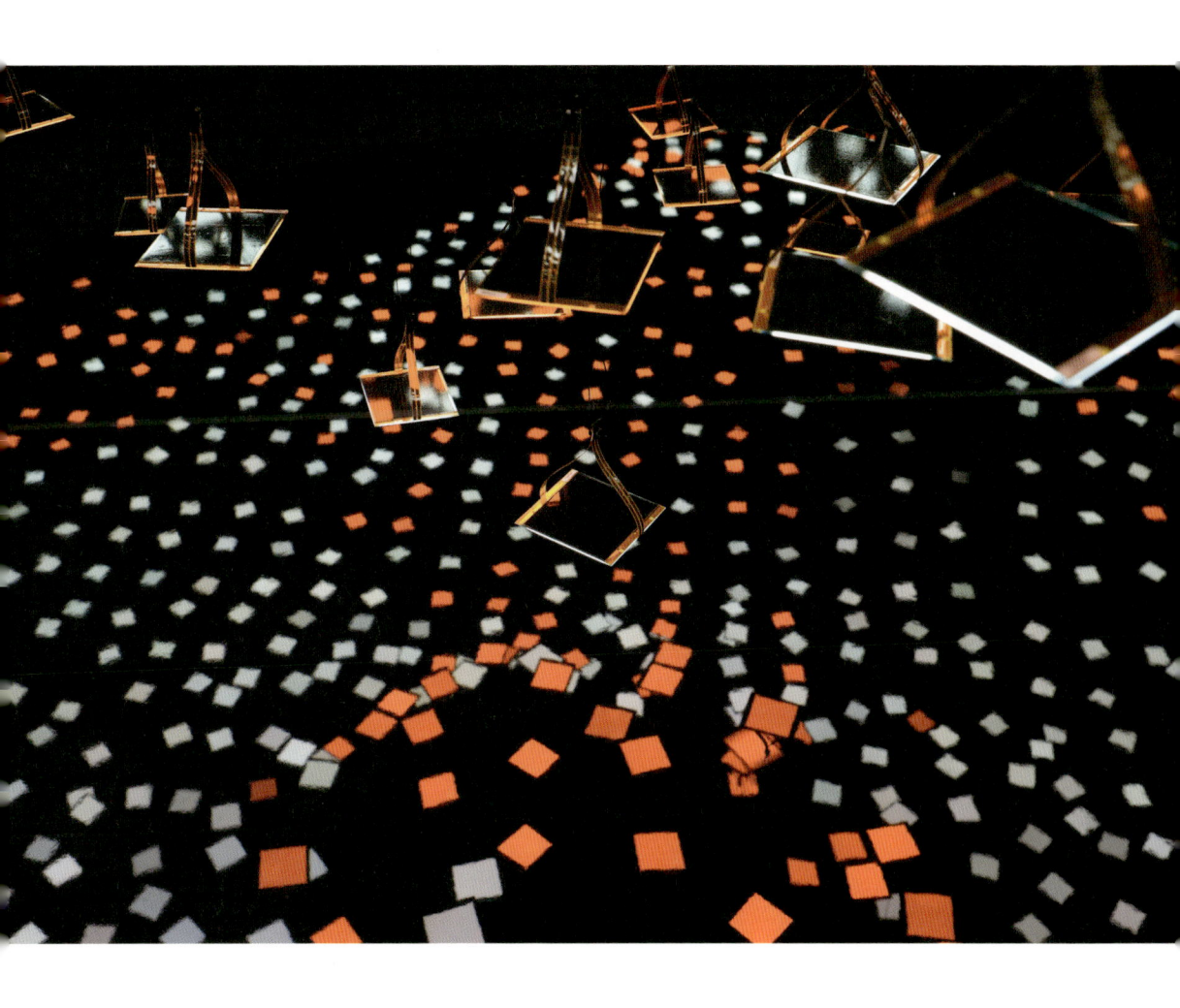

Inspired by flower basins, the counters were painted with a mirror finish to reflect the countless light surfaces. Programmed by light modulators, the OLED panels flicker organically.

水盤をイメージしたカウンターは塗装による鏡面仕上げで、無数の光の面を映し込む。OLEDパネルはプログラム調光で有機的な明滅を繰り返す。

MATERIALS AND GRAPHICS

GREGORY TOKYO STORE
GREGORY TOKYO STORE / 2008

A Forest, a Rock Wall and a Mountain Hut in Harajuku

Outdoor apparel maker Gregory opened its first road-side store in Harajuku's Cat Street. The 1F carries casual items such as bags, while professional mountain climbing gear can be found on the 2F. Since the existing building is located on the corner of a Y-intersection, it had no depth, so we had to make attempts at exhibiting a variety of products while giving adequate space for stock items in the limited site area.
We envisioned various settings; a ragged mountain, a dense forest and an Alpine hut to rest in, all of which Gregory backpacks have been utilized in. We set the hut behind the entrance's glass wall, which functions as the store's front display. Customers exiting the hut can see the store's lineup displayed on shelves that completely cover the wall. The backpacks lodged between the partition boards remind us of a rock climbing scene.

原宿に現れた森と岩壁と山小屋

原宿・キャットストリートにあるアウトドアブランド、グレゴリー初の路面店。1階はカジュアルなバッグなどのアイテム、2階は本格的な登山用商品という構成になっている。Y字路のコーナーという先細りした敷地のため、既存建物には奥行きがない。豊富な商品バリエーションを見せ、ストックを確保しながら、いかに特徴的な陳列をするかが問われた。
そこで、グレゴリー・バックパックの舞台となってきたごつごつとした岩山、生い茂った森林、休息のための山小屋といったモチーフによって各所の陳列方法を構成していった。山小屋が建物の吹き抜けに挿入され、入口のガラス壁で切り取られた室内の風景がストアの正面ディスプレイとなる。
小屋の内部から出るように進むと、岩肌の並ぶ"外部"となり、ラインナップが一望できる陳列棚が壁一面に展開する。仕切り板の合間から見えるバックパックの商品は、ロッククライミングのシーンのように見えてくる。

GREGORY TOKYO STORE

Trees are reflected on the mirrors outside. This forest made from reflections leads to the entrance to the 2F.
2階入口。手前にある木々が外壁面のミラーに映りこみ、森の中に入っていくイメージとなっている。

The exterior walls look like carved out rocks, functioning as a symbol of the Gregory store. (p.102)
岩肌のように荒々しい外壁は、そのたたずまい自体がサインとしても機能する。入口の木でできた部分が切り取られた"山小屋" (p.102)。

Mirrors on both ends of the shop create a continuous ragged mountain scenery. Stock items can be placed behind those displayed in front.
店内の両端にあるミラーは岩壁のように連続した風景をつくり出す。また、仕切り板は奥行きを持ち、狭小な空間において陳列とストックの機能を併せ持つ。

MATERIALS AND GRAPHICS

NIKE 1LOVE

NIKE 1LOVE / 2007

NIKE 1LOVE

We proposed to initially display only white Air Force 1's (p.104), which would gradually be replaced by new models that have reached the end of their sales period.

ガラスの円形ショーケースには、初めは真っ白いシューズが並べられ (p.104)、毎月出るニューモデルの販売期間が終わると、それらと入れ替えて展示される。

MATERIALS AND GRAPHICS

Aquarium of Migratory Air Force 1's

The NIKE "Air Force 1" store is a temporary showroom where new products are introduced each month over a period of one year. We intended for the customers to be able to visually enjoy the process in which the number of the products increases to no less than about 300.
To achieve this, we designed a double-glass cylindrical showcase where the lineup of initially white Air Force 1's gain colors as new models are released. The shoes all face the same direction, so that they look like a migratory school of fish swimming in an aquarium. And the look of this "school of shoes" changes as shoes of different colors are added to the tank.
On the 2F is a reservation only lounge where you can custom order your own original Air Force 1's. Looking down at the showcase through an opening that is surrounded by blue carpet, a school of Air Force 1's can be seen swimming underneath.

「Air Force 1」の回遊水族館

NIKEの「Air Force 1」(AF1)というシューズを専門に扱う1年間限定ストア。毎月増えていく新商品は最終的に300足近い数になり、その過程を視覚的に楽しめることが求められた。
ガラスの円形ショーケースに、初めは真っ白いAF1を並べ、ニューモデルがリリースされるたびに、順次入れ替え、色が付いていく。二重にしたガラスのシリンダー状のショーケースの中で、同じ向きで展示されるシューズが、水族館の水槽の中を回遊しているように計画した。このシューズの群れは、別の色を持ったシューズが交じることによって少しずつ、表情を変えていく。
2階はオリジナルのAF1をオーダーできる予約制ラウンジである。吹き抜けから1階のショーケース内を見下ろすと、水面に見立てた青いカーペット越しに、AF1の"群れ"がぐるぐると漂っている。

Silhouettes of swimming Air Force 1. (top)
The store is located along "Cat Street" in Harajuku, Tokyo. (bottom)
床に落ちるAF1のシルエット（上）。
原宿・キャットストリート沿いに建つ（下）。

Inspired by Air Force 1's pivot sole, the double-glass cylindrical showcase can be accessed by a sliding door. (p.107)
AF1のアウトソールに刻まれたピボットをモチーフにしたショーケース。二重ガラスの内側のガラスがスライドし、商品の入れ替えができる (p.107)。

NIKE 1LOVE

MATERIALS AND GRAPHICS

On the walls, we used white cemented excelsior boards to placard promotional materials such as posters. Its rough texture contrasts with the plain surface of the glass showcase. (top)

壁面は、ポスターなどの販促品の下地として、白塗装した木毛セメント板を張り、ハードな使い方のできる粗い表情とした。ガラスショーケースの平滑な表情と対比させている（上）。

The custom order lounge is fitted with a watery blue carpet while the shelves on the wall repeat the pivot sole motif. (bottom)

2階の予約制ラウンジ。壁面の棚造作もソールのピボットをモチーフにした。水面に見立てた青いカーペットを用いている（下）。

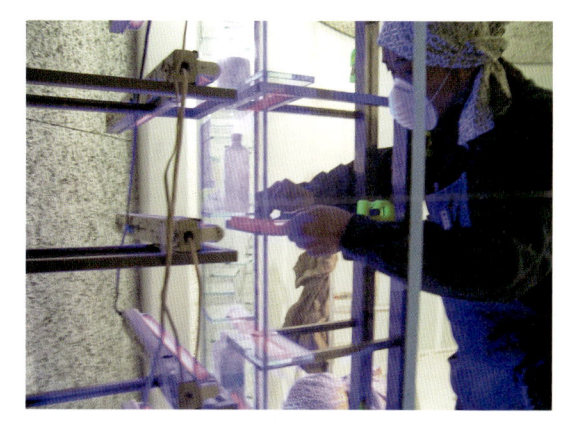

Shoes are displayed on high transmittance glass bracket shelves machined to fit the outer cylinder's curve and jointed with photobond, which hardens under ultraviolet rays; Installing the 4.3m wide glass cylinder.

シューズを載せる高透過ガラスのブラケット棚は、シリンダー外側のガラス曲面に、紫外線で硬化する接着剤で固定される。カーブの曲率に合わせ、棚板も加工されている。シリンダーの外径は4.3mになる。

MATERIALS AND GRAPHICS

CARBON HOLDER

炭素ホルダー / 2009

Carbon within Carbon

This leadholder design brings the carbon pipe material to life. Consisting of a soft graphite lead core wrapped in an ultra resistant carbon fiber sheath, we focused on bringing out the similarity between the black luster of the holder and that of the lead, as well as capitalizing on the material's strength. A simple concept that gives the sensation of holding a bare piece of pencil lead in one's hand.

炭素で炭素を包む

カーボンパイプの素地を活かした、芯ホルダーのデザイン。炭素素材の柔らかい芯が、高強度の炭素繊維素材に覆われている。カーボンの持つ強度と鉛筆の芯のように黒光りする表情の類似性に注目した。あたかも芯そのものを手にしているような、シンプルなホルダーである。

SKY HOUSE

スカイハウス / 2006

A House View Made from Houses

We designed the facade for the "100 Solutions ROOM" exhibition site. Since the concept of the exhibition is to offer 100 different ideas for living, we proposed a huge house-shaped facade composed of hundreds of small houses. The exhibition can be seen from the street through the house's windows, while the view from the inside juxtaposes a pattern of small houses to the familiar scenery.

家が構成する家の風景

「100 Solutions ROOM」という企画展示のファサード計画。100の暮らしのアイデアを見せるという企画から、たくさんの小さな家のグラフィックで大きな家型のファサードを提案した。通りからは"家の窓"越しに展示を見ることができ、内部からは、街並みと小さな家によるパターンが重なり、見慣れた風景が一変する。

4

SUGGESTIONS FOR AN OFFICE SPACE
オフィススペースへの提案

Working at the right kind of space, will allow invisible things such as ambitions and ideals inherent to the company to naturally emerge.

そこで働く人たちにふさわしい空間には、
会社というものが備える、
目には見えない意欲や理念のようなものが
自然と表れてくる。

SUGGESTIONS FOR AN OFFICE SPACE

NIKE JMC
NIKE JMC / 2009

NIKE JMC

Bringing Out the Scale of a Large Space

We designed NIKE's offices and exhibition space in a way that would make the best use of the building's characteristics. The renovated storehouse has 5 floors, each at 6m high, representing a total floor space of 5600m² distributed between a merchandising space on the 1F, a hall on the 2F, exhibition spaces on the 3F and 4F with storage space on the 5F.
In order to do so, we left the large spaces completely intact and pondered at length on the elements to be included or removed. The cemented excelsior boards used for the walls, the recycled scrap wood flooring used in the furniture and the court lines on the floor are all elements found in a gymnasium. We tried to bring out the scale of the existing building frame and recreate the looks of a stadium by applying the names of important rooms in large letters directly on the walls.
By matching the materials found in the existing ceiling with that of the new walls, we set out to blur the distinction between old & new, before & after and ultimately emphasize their equivalence.

大空間のスケールを活かす

NIKEの展示スペースとオフィス機能を併設する施設。階高6m、5階建て、延床面積5600㎡という規模で、もともと物流倉庫であった建物をリノベーションして使用する。その特長を活かし、ブランドとしてアピールできる空間を求められた。1階にはマーチャンダイジングスペース、2階にはホール、3階と4階は展示会のためのスペース、5階は倉庫という構成になっている。
広大な空間の設計において、残す要素と付加する要素の選択を慎重に行った。体育館などで使用される木毛セメント板による壁面、同じく体育館の廃材フローリングによる家具、床面のコートラインなど、スポーツの大空間にちなんで部分を決定していく。空間のスケール感を活かし、主要な室名はスタジアムのサインのように大きく直接壁面へ施した。
既存の天井面と新規壁面の素材の一致など、新しいものと古いものの前後関係が倒錯し、それぞれが対等に存在する状態を目指した。

SUGGESTIONS FOR AN OFFICE SPACE

The 2F and upper levels feature exhibition and meeting rooms. Areas found between existing walls are converted into lounges to maximize space usage.
2階より上のフロアには、展示スペースや会議室など諸機能を配した。既存の壁面との余白はラウンジとして利用している。

Names of rooms and floors are applied on walls. Different color schemes provide guidance to occupants.
壁面に直接書かれた室名やサイン。所々にある差し色を与えられた空間が人を誘導する。

SUGGESTIONS FOR AN OFFICE SPACE

Mesh panels for displaying products were installed over the curving walls made from cemented excelsior boards.
木毛セメント板による湾曲した壁面には、商品をディスプレイするためのメッシュパネルが帯状に連なる。

The 1F lobby's furniture can be rearranged to create a flexible space in the image of a sports arena. The table on casters in the foreground is a collage of planks taken from the floor of a gymnasium.

1階にあるマーチャンダイジングスペースは、可動式の家具が置かれ、スポーツフィールドのようなフレキシブルな空間とした。手前の可動テーブルは、解体された体育館の床板をコラージュして製作した。

SUGGESTIONS FOR AN OFFICE SPACE

The 1F lobby. Artist Takeshi Abe utilized a portrait picture of NIKE's founder to create this wall artwork made with 2cm cubes placed side by side. (top)

1階ロビー。壁面のアートワークは、NIKE創設者の顔写真を用いてアーティストの阿部岳史が2cm角の立方体を並べ制作(上)。

The hall on the 2F is used for seminars and events. The extensive scale of this distribution warehouse was put to good use. (bottom left)

2階のセミナー兼イベント用のホール。広大な物流倉庫のスケールを活かした(左下)。

The 1F lobby counter. Select materials make the furniture look attractive, with the coarse grain of larch plywood contrasting against the industrial impression of the building. (bottom right)

1階ロビーのカウンター。工業的な印象の既存建物に対し、ラーチ合板の粗い木目による家具が映える(右下)。

NIKE JMC

SIGN: SPACES

BLAZER
HERITAGE
NIKE+
T90
KNIGHT'S
HALL

SIGN: TOILETS

MEN　WOMEN　MEN　WOMEN　MEN　WOMEN

SIGN: LEVELS

1 2 3 4

Typeface and pictograms designed specifically for this facility. "TAKAI-YAMA inc." was in charge of the signage design.

この施設のためにつくられたサインの書体とピクトグラム。デザインは「高い山」が担当。

SUGGESTIONS FOR AN OFFICE SPACE

1-10design Kyoto Office

1→10design 京都オフィス / 2011

Partitions That Flow into Each Other

仕切りながら
ゆるやかにつながる

The office of Kyoto-based web production company, 1-10design (one to ten design), comprises of a single 460m² versatile area featuring work spaces, a meeting room, a gallery and a traditional Japanese room which serves as a resting area.
We proposed a spacious floor finely partitioned by wooden frames, allowing rooms of various sizes to flow into each other. The framework can also serve as shelves on which we can find office furnishings alongside personal belongings. The frames keep functional spaces separated as the rooms' appearance change every time one passes through them, and yet offer a peering view that gives the whole floor a sense of continuity.
This bare skeleton can become a wall as much as it can become a piece of furniture, but it really serves as a background, prompting miscellaneous interactions by keeping the ability to accommodate future changes with flexibility. The office allows one to change the scene in front of us according to our mood while preserving the sense of unity of a single room.

京都を拠点に活動しているウェブプロダクション1→10design（ワン・トゥー・テン・デザイン）のオフィス内装計画。460㎡ほどのワンルームに、ワークスペース、ミーティングルーム、ギャラリーや休憩のための和室など、多種の用途が求められた。
これらの用途と、オフィス用品や個人の所有物を収容するため、棚としても使える木の格子が広いフロアを細かく仕切り、大小の室が連続していく空間を提案した。格子の仕切りをくぐるたびに場面が切り替わり、各用途を仕切りながらも視線が通り、フロア全体につながりを持たせている。
壁であると同時に家具でもある、骨組みだけの木の格子は、さまざまな行為のきっかけを与える背景のような役目を持ち、今後の変化にも柔軟に対応することができる。ワンルームの一体感を保ちながら、気分によって場面を切り替えることができるようなオフィスを目指した。

The main workspace, located in the center, extends over several rooms. A long table crosses the whole length as though it were connecting all the separate rooms together. (p.120)

メインのワークスペースは複数の室にまたがって中央に位置し、長いテーブルがばらばらの室をつなぎとめるように全体を横断する (p.120)。

The wooden lattice is made to be a flexible construction that, depending on the location, serves alternately as bookshelf and storage space, message board and bench.

木の格子は場所によって本棚や収納、掲示板、ベンチといったさまざまな使い方ができるフレキシブルな仕組みをあわせ持つ。

SUGGESTIONS FOR AN OFFICE SPACE

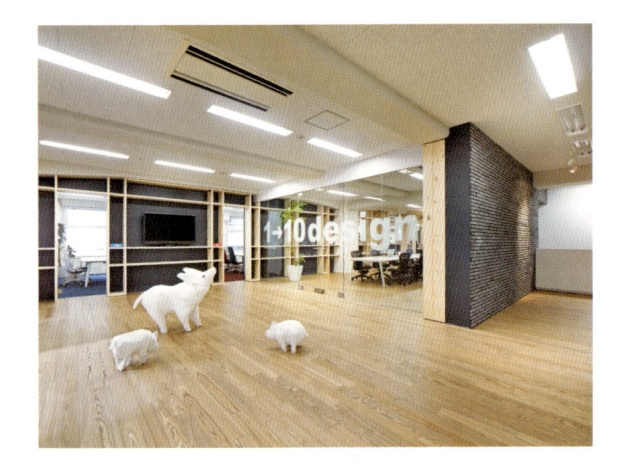

The entrance. It also serves as a meeting place gallery to exhibit works of art.
エントランス。アート作品が展示される、待合のためのギャラリーにもなっている。

Each room is loosely connected but also divided by the lattice.
各部屋は格子で仕切られつつも、ゆるやかにつながっている。

A Japanese-style room lies at the end of the stone path after passing through the *Noren* (curtain-like cloths).
石畳の奥の暖簾をくぐり和室へ入る。

1-10design Kyoto Office

Looking back at the entrance from the office interior.
オフィスの奥からエントランス方向を見返す。

An overhead view of a model showing interconnected rooms of various sizes.
模型の俯瞰。大小の室が連続する。

SUGGESTIONS FOR AN OFFICE SPACE

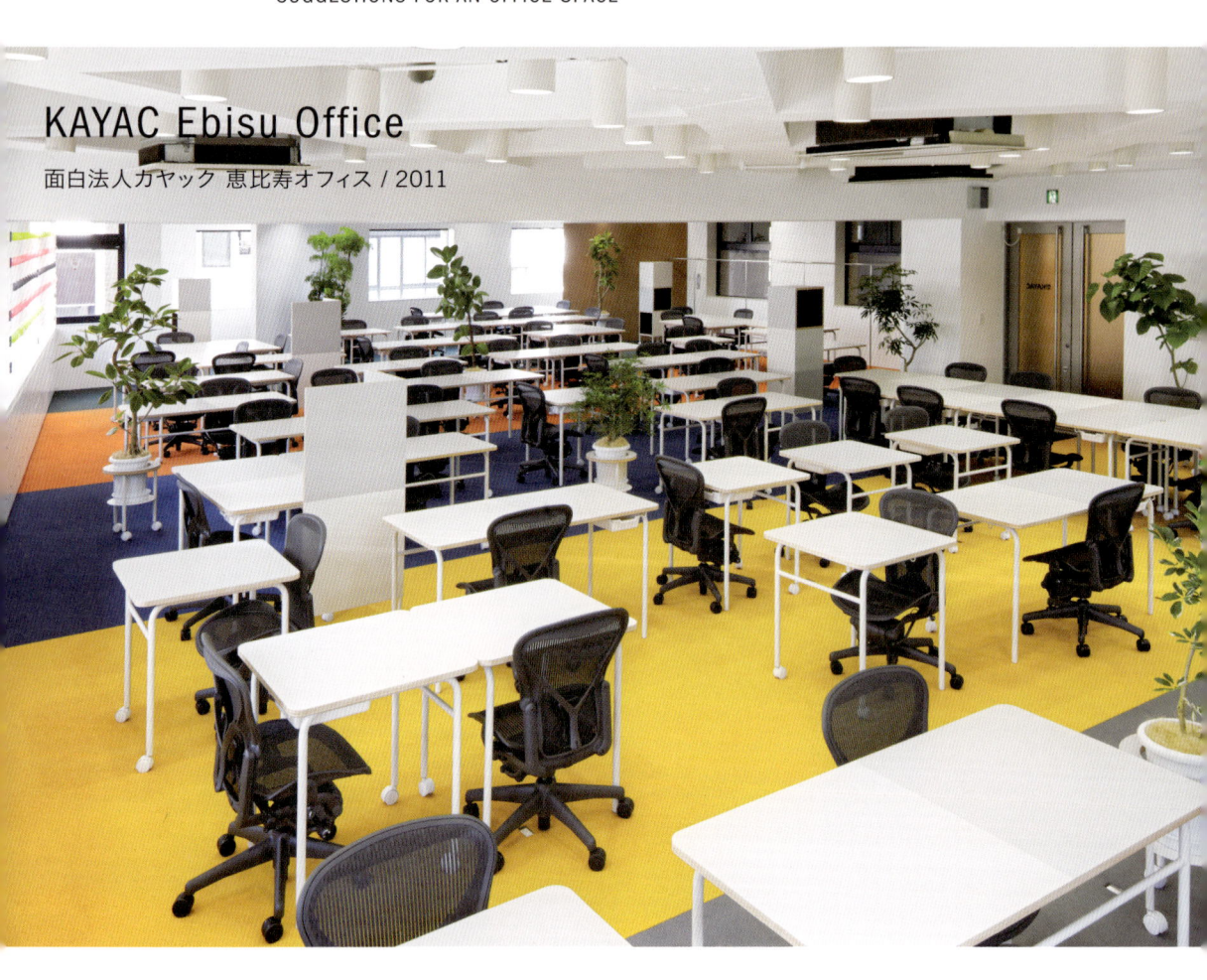

KAYAC Ebisu Office
面白法人カヤック 恵比寿オフィス / 2011

A Variable Office Space That Can Be Freely Configured

KAYAC is an IT business that is also into the idea of a "Fun-loving Business". For their new Tokyo branch office, we thought of a space with the flexibility to adapt to changes where employees could enjoy visualizing their company's performance. Since project teams need to change constantly and fluidly, so do the desk layouts in the office. We thus proposed an office with adaptable features that offers each member a private desk which can be reshuffled at will into a temporary configuration and accommodate for future additions to the team. The side facing the entrance features windows and a wall where each month's corporate performance can be visualized. Employees themselves can update the ledger daily with colored balls on a mesh to show sales as they are being made.
By giving the office a flexible configuration that does not overly monopolize the entire space, and by keeping the corporate performance results in the field of vision at all times, we sought to fit out the company's new working space in the same way as they are proposing their new style of working to others.

自由に組み替える 可変的オフィス

面白法人カヤックの東京支社の内装計画。ITビジネスを根幹とする同社の新オフィスには、業績の達成度を社員が楽しめる仕掛けを用意することと、変化に対応するフレキシビリティーを求められた。
プロジェクトのチーム編成が流動的なため、デスクレイアウトには常に変化が求められる。また今後の人員増加への対応も考慮して、デスクを一人に一つずつ割り当て、自由に組み替えることのできる可変的な特性を持ったオフィスを提案した。
入って正面の窓面側には、月ごとの業績をカラーボールでビジュアル化する壁面を設置。常に視界に入る会社の業績と、すべてを決め付けすぎない柔軟な仕組みによって、ワークスタイルそのものを提案する企業のオフィスとしてフィットするよう考えた。

KAYAC Ebisu Office

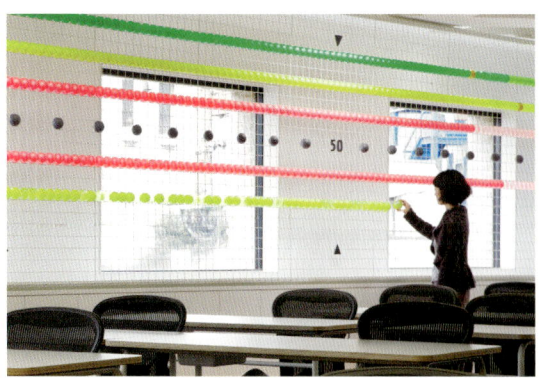

A fluid, mobile office unrestrained by fixed furniture thanks to the casters that have been applied like roller-skates to the desks, shelves, partitions and planters. (p.124)

デスク、シェルフ、パーティション、プランターにもローラースケートを履かせるようにキャスターを取り付けて可動性を持たせることで、固定家具にしばられない流動的なオフィスとした (p.124)。

The colored balls that employees insert into the mesh screen represent what sales units have become and are updated daily. The colorful, ever-changing graph helps to liven up the space. (bottom left)

社員自らがメッシュのスクリーンにはめ込むカラーボールが売上の単位となり日々更新されていく。常に変化するカラフルなグラフが空間を彩っている (左下)

SUGGESTIONS FOR AN OFFICE SPACE

UDS Shanghai Office
UDS 上海オフィス / 2005

UDS Shanghai Office

The light from outside is reflected by the mirrors and the shadows they cast behind them produce an exquisite pattern on the floor, constantly changing the look of the whole office according to time.

ガラス越しの風景と、ミラーに映り込む手前の風景とが同一平面上に混在する。外光によって、ミラーに反射した光とその裏側に落とす影とが美しい模様を織り成し、絶えず変化する光景を生む。

SUGGESTIONS FOR AN OFFICE SPACE

A Boundary Surface Where Images Interplay

This is an interior design project for UDS' Shanghai branch, which is involved in building corporative housing in China. UDS requested there to be a workspace for their business partners that would mitigate sound and gazes from the outside. Dividing up the 86m² office could make it feel very narrow, so we proposed the use of mirrors with a striped pattern in order to not only divide the office space but make it look larger at the same time. The view through the glass and the reflections lining alternately on one plane surface, blur the distinction between real and virtual images. This seemingly confusing scenery brings together these opposing realities, resembling Shanghai's own paradoxical landscape.

像が交錯する境界面

コーポラティブハウスなどを手掛けてきた都市デザインシステム (UDS) の中国上海支店オフィスの内装計画。打ち合わせ室など来客のための空間と執務空間とは音や視線を遮ることが要求された。
86m²ほどの小さなオフィスを仕切ると、とても狭く感じてしまう。そこで、分節しながらも視覚的に拡大する境界面をつくり出す方法として、ストライプ状の模様を持つミラーで仕切ることを提案した。
透明なガラス越しの風景と、ミラーに映り込む手前の風景とが同一平面上に交互に現れ、実像と虚像が倒錯したような感覚を与える。その混在した風景はあたかも、対立的なものが隣り合わせになっている上海の風景を思わせる。

The mirror stripes give the illusion that your reflection is talking with other people in the room across the screen. (p.129 top)

ミラーで映り込み、増幅した自分の分身と、ガラスの向こう側で別の人と会話をしているかのような錯覚を抱かせる (p.129上)。

The back of the mirrors are painted in white to blend with the wall, so people passing outside can be seen through the stripes. (p.129 middle)

ストライプ状のミラー面の裏側は白く塗られ、壁と同化して人の行き来を垣間見ることができる (p.129中)。

The desks, placed along the walls, cross both spaces like a belt, further blurring the distinction between real and virtual images. (p.129 bottom)

デスクは、間仕切りをまたぎ、壁伝いに一周する帯のような形状とした。仕切られた両方の空間を横断していることから、実像と虚像の交錯をさらに強める (p.129下)。

UDS Shanghai Office

SUGGESTIONS FOR AN OFFICE SPACE

DWJ Office

DWJ Office / 2007

An Underwater-like Wobble and Transparency

These are the offices of Danone Waters of Japan (DWJ), who imports, distributes and sells bottled mineral water products. They have workspaces for approximately 30 employees and 8 conference rooms in 962m² of the estate. The conference room needed to represent water and be expansive while mitigating sound and view from the outside.
We proposed a clear and transparent space as to make us feel depth and at the same time appear visually partitioned by the refraction of water. Each partition is made of 1000 glass rods 60mm across and represents the shape of big water drops. As light permeates the glass, the scenery is reflected on the surface and the image is distorted. By introducing the wavering, clearness and fluidity that water represents into the workspace, we hoped the scenery through the glass tubes will make workers, who spend most of their day in the office, feel the transition of time.

水の中にいるようなゆらぎと透明感

ミネラルウォーターの輸入・流通・販売を行うダノンウォーターズオブジャパン（DWJ）のオフィス。962m²というスペースに、30人ほどの社員のワークスペースと八つのミーティングルームなどを持つ。ミーティングルームには視線や音を遮りながらもオープンな空間であること、水を扱うDWJらしさが表現されていることが求められた。
そこで、透明で奥行きを感じられつつ、水の屈折のようにゆがみによって視覚的に分節されている空間を提案した。直径60mmのガラス管約1000本の集合による間仕切りが、水滴をイメージした曲率の違う自由な平面形を実現させている。
連続するガラス管によって、光は通過し、風景が映り込み、像はゆがむ。1日の多くをオフィスで過ごす社員に、水のゆらぎのような風景は時の移ろいを感じさせる。ゆらぎや透明感、流動性など、水の液体としての物性を空間に取り込み計画した。

DWJ Office

SUGGESTIONS FOR AN OFFICE SPACE

The display at the entrance looks like a water drop dripping down from the big glass rods.

エントランス脇のディスプレイ什器は、ガラス管による大きな円形から分離したしずくをイメージした。

Wavy entrances leading to the central utility space make us feel as if we ourselves were wavering in the water.

ワークスペース中央に位置するユーティリティスペースの開口も、水中で揺らいでいるかのようなゆがんだ形状とした。

DWJ Office

We colored the carpet as to mismatch the partition lines on the floor and to boost the feeling of wavering water. The ceiling was painted to make it look as if the color of the floor was reflected on it.

水滴が揺れているような印象を与えるため、床のカーペットは間仕切りのガラス管のラインとずらして色を変えた。天井はその床の色が反射して映り込んでいるかのように、繊細に着色した。

Glass tubes (5mm thick, 60mm across, 2580mm long) were produced in China. Silicone gaskets were inserted between neighboring glass tubes to block sound.

ガラス管は、厚さ5mm、直径60mmで、長さは2580mm。すべて中国で製作された。音を遮るため、隣り合う管の間にシリコンを挟み込んで、上下のスチール枠をガイドにして設置している。

COLUMN 02

TORAFU AND MATERIALS
トラフと素材

The whole town is like a catalogue of samples

Torafu selects and stocks everyday materials that they find interesting. All of these various accumulated materials are like treasures to them. That being said, these materials are used to offer a new perspective rather than simply building something based off of them. In other words, these are literally samples that are used to make people aware of the way they see things and to transform their way of thinking. Of course, it is also possible to arrive at a new conception when looking at samples and wondering what can be done with them.
At the "UDS Shanghai Office" (p.126), they thought it would be interesting to bring striped and silver plated glass that they had created in the past and connect it to their proposal for partitions.
"No matter how clear the concept is, carelessness shown towards the details of the materials and the end product will cause disappointment when people see the result. We don't want to create something that will destroy the concept".
Torafu is always prudent in handling materials that have a connection to the design interface and people's emotions.

The office carries a large stock of samples.
事務所にストックされているたくさんの素材サンプル。

Mirror glass sheets with stripe patterns used at the "UDS Shanghai Office".
「UDS 上海オフィス」で使われた、ストライプのミラーガラス。

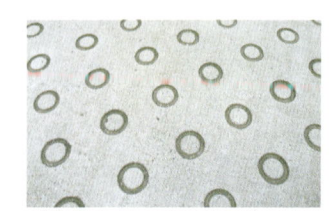

Anti-slip rings found on roads became the inspiration for "RING PARKING" (p.174).
「リング バーキング」(p.174)のヒントになった路面の滑り止め。

Reflective material used on pavement at the "GREGORY TOKYO STORE" (p.102) made to look like minerals in a rocky mountain.
舗装用の反射材を「GREGORY TOKYO STORE」(p.102)では岩山の鉱石に見立てた。

街中がサンプル帳のようにも見える

トラフは、日常でも面白いと思える素材はピックアップし、ストックしている。そうして集められたさまざまな素材は彼らにとっては宝物だという。とはいってもあくまでも素材にすぎず、それありきで何かをつくり出すというよりは、"新しい視点を提供できるようにするための素材"、つまりそこからモノの見方や発想の転換に気付いてもらうための、文字通り「サンプル」である。もちろん、逆にサンプルを見ながら、ここから何かできないか、と新しい発想につながることもある。
「UDS 上海オフィス」(p.126)では、面白いと思って以前につくっておいたストライプ状に銀引きされた板ガラスのサンプルを持って、パーティションの提案に結び付けた。
「コンセプトがどんなに鮮やかでも、素材のディテールや納まりがおろそかだとそれを見た瞬間にさめてしまう。"コンセプト倒れ"のようにはしたくない」
それだけに、デザインのインターフェースや人の感情につながる素材の扱いには、常に思慮を巡らしている。

TORAFU AND MATERIALS

COLUMN 02

Taking a flat look at materials

Creating interest by displaying premium materials in a flimsy manner... Finding something fresh by slightly tweaking the kind of mass-produced objects that are normally used in the background. Torafu's approach is to draw out the qualities of each material without getting caught up in the hierarchy of cost and performance.

For example, there are the wood wool cement (cemented excelsior) boards used on the interior walls of the store "NIKE 1LOVE". (p.104) Using a roller to paint them white gives a less woody impression but still leaves a coarse texture. This creates a contrast with the delicate, sharp glass showcase and helps to bring out a greater sense of depth within that space. Moreover, it also adds significant functionality by making it easier to attach posters, exhibit items, and so on.

At the "HermanMiller Store Tokyo" (p.64), a variety of floor materials have been placed in a pattern around the store so that people can imagine how the store's products would be used in various situations. At first glance it almost resembles a decorative sheet, but it is the marble, the carpet and the flooring that really provide a sense of texture and feel for the materials. Treating everything graphically produces a sense of marvel and colorful fun.

素材はフラットに見る

高級な素材をあえて薄っぺらく見せることで生まれる面白さ——。裏方で使われるような大量生産品に少しだけ手を加えることで見える新鮮さ。価格や性能というヒエラルキーにとらわれずに、それぞれの素材のよさを探し出すというのがトラフの姿勢だ。

例えば「NIKE 1LOVE」(p.104)で店内の壁面に使われている木毛セメント板。ローラーで白く塗るともとの木質系の印象は薄れ、一方で粗いテクスチャーは残る。精緻でシャープなガラスのショーケースとのコントラストを生み、空間の表情に奥行きが出る。また、ポスターや展示品を貼り付けやすいなど、機能的にも意味がある。

「ハーマンミラーストア東京」(p.64)では、置かれる製品のシチュエーションを想像できるよう、さまざまな床の素材を、パターンのように店内にちりばめている。一見、それらはまるで化粧シートのようでいて、実際の感触と質感を備えた大理石やカーペットやフローリングだ。あえてグラフィカルに扱うことで印象の不思議さ、彩りの楽しさも提供する。

Cemented excelsior boards are made of compacted ribbons of wood mixed with cement.
木毛セメント板はリボン状の木材をセメントに混ぜ込んで、圧縮成型したもの。

The boards were used on the 1F walls and ceiling of "NIKE 1LOVE".
「NIKE 1LOVE」では、1階の壁と天井に使った。

The flooring at the "HermanMiller Store Tokyo" is made of natural wood arranged in a herringbone pattern and laid out like carpet.
無垢材をヘリンボーン貼りしたフローリングも、「ハーマンミラーストア東京」では敷き物のように扱った。

COLUMN 02

Neutrality is convenient

Among all the common materials, Torafu often use wooden boards – MDF (medium-density fiberboard) and OSB (structural panels). They prefer MDF that is non-directional, does not have wood grain, and is not hung up on the symbolic characteristics of a tree.

At the HOUSE IN KOHOKU (p.44), the concrete framework that combines the outer walls and roof is like a shell, while the interior design of the floor and furniture, all of which consist of MDFs with a paint finish, creates the impression of being natural by-products of the floor. Since the edges and board surface of the MDFs are identical, they appear to be one body. These kinds of wooden boards are very convenient in terms of cost and performance, but their aspect is derived from their manufacturing method and function that is not intended to be decorative.

"When you use wood that has a rich grain and aspect, the meaning and reason behind it will be questioned. We don't want to use it for such reasons as it gives a warm impression, etc".

In this sense, neutral materials are much more convenient. Unnecessary emphasis can actually become an obstruction in terms of design.

The floor and furniture in the "HOUSE IN KOHOKU" is made of MDF.
床も家具もMDFで統一した「港北の住宅」。

The circular cases of "SPINNING OBJECTS" are coated in urethane to conceal the MDF material.
「回転体」(p.68)の什器は、素材感を出さないようMDFにウレタン塗装を重ね塗りした。

We were involved in designing the office interior for "ReBITA" (2005). We applied a versatile material on one surface of these boxes made with neutral-looking MDF.
オフィスの内装を手掛けた「リビタ」(2005年)では、MDFでニュートラルなボックスをつくり、一面のみに多彩な素材を貼った。

ニュートラルさが使いやすい

一般的な素材の中ではいわゆる木質系ボード――MDF（中質繊維板）やOSB（構造用パネル）などを用いることが多い。MDFは、「方向性や木目がなく、木の記号性にとらわれないところ」を好んでいる。

「港北の住宅」(p.44)では、コンクリートの躯体ですべてが一体になった外壁、天井をシェルのように例え、それを受ける内装の床や造作家具はすべてMDFの染色仕上げとして、床から派生してきたようなイメージでつくっている。MDFは小口も板面も同じ表層を持っているため、一つの塊のように見える。こうした木質系ボードは、価格や性能としては木材並みに使いやすい一方、その表情は製法や機能から出てきているもので、装飾的な意図はない。

「木目や表情の豊かな木材を使うと、その意味や理由を求められてしまう。なんとなく温かいイメージがある、という理由だけでは使いたくない」という。あくまでもニュートラルな方が使いやすい。不必要な主張はデザインする上で、妨げになる場合もある。

Capitalizing on the strength of collaborators

At "NIKE 1LOVE", one of the main issues in regard to advancing the project was the manner in which they would achieve the realization of a large glass showcase. By pure chance, Mihoya Glass decided to join the project. This glass company billed itself as a "glass maker for the design industry" due to its experience with creating special-order glass for use in the works of famous designers and artists. Mihoya Glass came to be known for its former collaboration with the designer Shiro Kuramata.

"Since they joined the project, we wanted to take advantage of their capabilities". The square shape that they had envisioned for the showcase at first changed to become a cylindrical shape. Covered in highly transparent glass with a sliding glass door, it almost resembles an aquarium. This showcase relates to the narrative of the "School of Air Force 1" swimming in circles. Aside from having an interest in the architecture or program, they were able to give this work greater depth so that more people could see it from a different perspective. It is very reassuring for Torafu to have the backup of such manufacturing / building contract companies. "This collaborative network is a great support when giving consideration to design".

This circular glass showcase would not have been possible without the help of collaborators.
コラボレーターの力なしでは実現しなかったガラスの円形ショーケース。

The "ORE-CHAIR" (2009) was designed for an exhibition held for the 100th anniversary of Mihoya Glass.
三保谷硝子店の100周年記念の展覧会のためにデザインした「オレチェア」(2009年)。

コラボレーターの力を活かす

「NIKE 1LOVE」(p.104)では、巨大なガラスのショーケースをいかに実現するかがプロジェクトを進める上で大きな課題となった。ところが、ひょんなことから三保谷硝子店がプロジェクトに参加することになった。同社は高名なデザイナーやアーティストの作品などに使われる特注ガラス製作を手掛け、"デザイン業界のガラス屋さん"を自称する。かつては倉俣史朗との協働で知られる。

「せっかく参加してもらうのであれば、その力を引き出していきたい」。当初、四角い形状を想定していたショーケースは円柱になり、湾曲したスライドガラス戸を備え、高透過ガラスで覆われ、さも水族館のような様子を湛えた。それがAir Force 1の群れが回遊するというストーリーに結び付く。建築的あるいはプログラムとしての面白さ以外に、多くの人が別の視点でとらえられる奥行きを作品に与えることができた。

このようにバックアップしてくれる製作・施工会社などの存在は心強いという。「コラボレーターたちとのネットワークがデザインを考える上でも大きな支えになっている」

We first experienced the fascination for form after we assembled the "MOUNTAIN DISPLAY" (2008), which was made by Inoue Industries.
「マウンテン ディスプレイ」(2008年)では什器が組み上がって初めてかたちの面白さが実感できた。製作はイノウエインダストリィズ。

COLUMN 02

Creating on the spot

Torafu often visits manufacturing sites and workshops. "There are many unfinished goods lined up in the workshop. We are interested in the stage just before a work is complete because it allows some room for people to get involved in the process". By stepping into the manufacturing process in this way, you are able to think more carefully about the work in its temporarily exposed state. From there it is possible to branch off and create something new, or make something look new by combining it with something else.

The "KIRIKO BOTTLE" (p.176) was created by utilizing traditional *Kiriko* cut glass techniques and combining it with regular milk bottles and soy sauce bottles.

The idea behind the EXHIBITION "bones" (p.168), which only displayed the framework of furniture, came about when they did a product check at a workshop and were struck by the structural beauty of the unfinished furniture.

"A new perspective on things that are already there... By providing such a way of thinking and seeing things, everything around us will feel like it has more depth".

This is tied in to the way we choose materials and the way we think about things. It gives us a chance to reexamine our lifestyle and the things surrounding us.

A masterpiece in the making by an Edo Kiriko artisan.
江戸切子の職人による見事な手業。

The unfinished structure found by chance during a product check at a furniture workshop.
製品チェックで訪れた家具工場でたまたま見た下地だけの家具。

The spherical display for the "DWJ Office" is made of FRP and smoothed by hand.
「DWJ Office」(p.130)のための球体ディスプレイ什器はFRPの本体を手作業で平滑にした。

現場から生み出される

トラフは製作の現場や工場にも足しげく訪れるようにしている。「工場には製品になる途中のものがたくさん並んでいて、そういうできあがる手前のところには人の入り込む余地があって興味をそそられる」

ものづくりのプロセスに介入していくことで、一旦バラした状態で考えてみることができる。そこから分岐して別のものになる可能性も生まれるし、別のものと組み合わせるだけで新鮮に見えてくることもある。

「キリコ ボトル」(p.176)ではすでに完成された伝統工芸である切子硝子の技術を、その技法だけに注目し、日常的に見ている牛乳ビンや醤油ビンに組み合わせた。

「『骨』展」(p.168)の骨組だけの什器は、家具工場で見た仕上げ前の家具の構造美にみせられたことを発端としている。

「すでにあるものの見え方が新しくなる。そういう考え方や視点を提供することで、まわりのいろいろなものが豊かに感じられる」素材の選び方は、ものの考え方につながる。ものや暮らしを見直してみるきっかけを与えてくれる。

5

A DESIGN ORIGINATING FROM A CONNECTION
かかわりから生まれるデザイン

A design that is first established based upon experience and content.

そこで行われる体験やコンテンツ、
それがあって初めて成立するデザインとは。

A DESIGN ORIGINATING FROM A CONNECTION

Run Pit by au Smart Sports
Run Pit by au Smart Sports / 2010

Run Pit by au Smart Sports

1F of the Palaceside Building facing the Imperial Palace moat.
皇居のお堀に面したパレスサイドビルの1階に位置する。

A DESIGN ORIGINATING FROM A CONNECTION

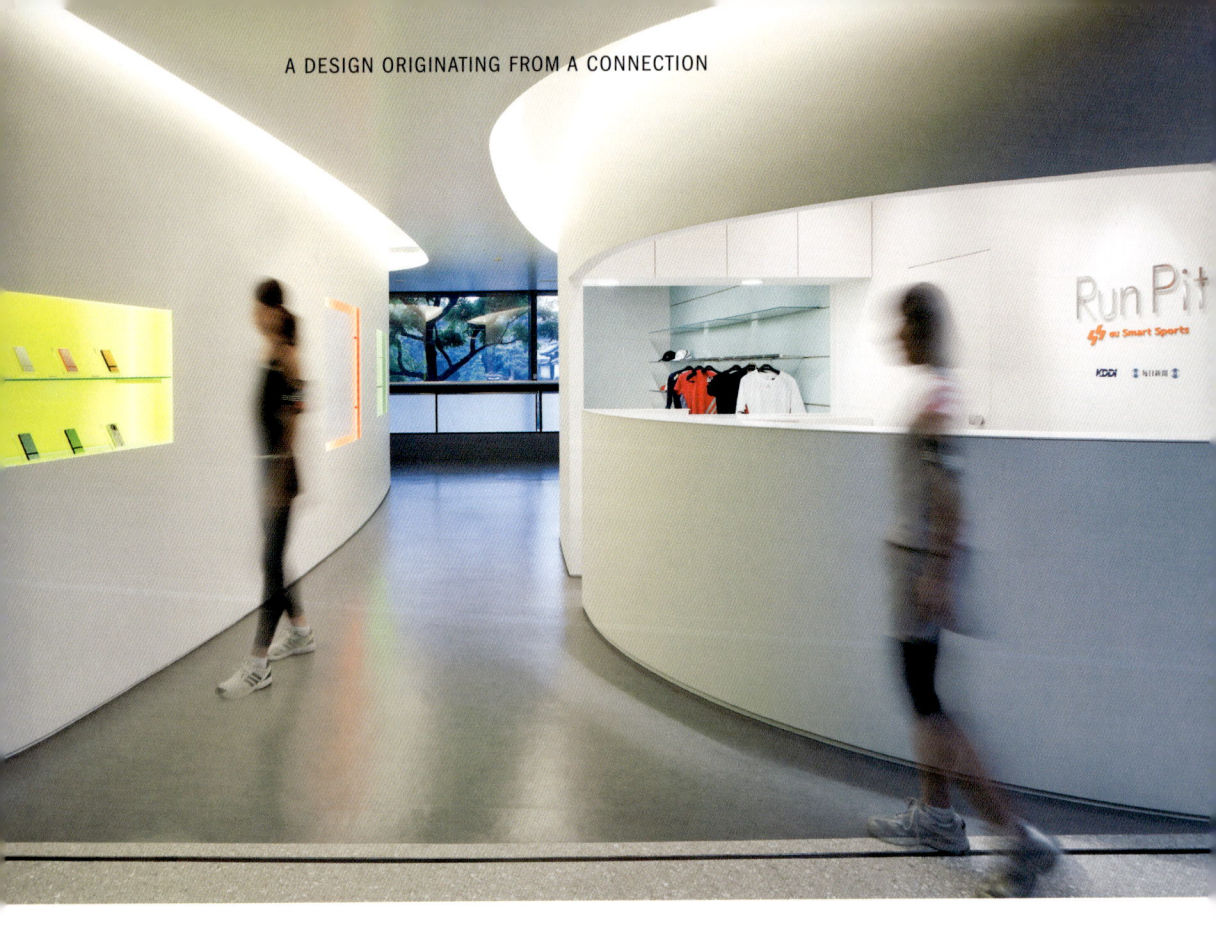

A Facility to Renovate Urban Functionality

Located in a corner of the Palaceside Building, the facility offers a meeting lounge, a boutique and locker rooms fitted with showers as well as an easy access to a 5km circuit around the Tokyo Imperial Palace. We proposed a tunnel-like space made of sinuous walls to serve as a multi-function showcase. At the junction between the men's and women's areas, the tunnel presents a great view on the green Imperial grounds through a window facing a long counter where runners can rendezvous or simply cool off. Behind the wavy walls we find the locker rooms, styled in well-appointed masculine and feminine tones. The interior of an office building poses a challenge of structural uniformity which we sought to alleviate by linking the inner and outer spaces and allowing the street to be experienced from within the structure as one big running track.

街の機能を更新する

皇居の周囲約5kmを走るランナーに向けた施設で、パレスサイドビル内の一角に、着替えのためのロッカースペース、シャワー設備、物販コーナーやラウンジスペースなどを併設する。
ここでは、ショーケースなどの諸機能を内包する湾曲した壁面によるトンネル状の空間を提案した。中央のトンネルを抜けると、緑豊かな皇居周辺の風景が広がる。その風景を望む窓いっぱいの長いカウンターを設け、休憩や待ち合わせのためのスペースとした。曲面壁で囲われた内部は、ロッカールームなど男女別のスペースで、それぞれを統一した色調で仕上げている。
建物内部ですべてのことが完結してしまいがちなオフィスビルの現状に対して、外を感じ、街とつながっていけるように提案した。小さな内装計画でありながら、この場所があることによって、街全体がランニングコースとして描きかえられたように見えてくる。

The entrance. Nested in the curving walls are showcases for products and a shop.
エントランス。ショーケースや物販コーナーが収められた湾曲した壁面。

Run Pit by au Smart Sports

The window-wide polished counter top and ceiling let in more of the scenery and nearby trees.

窓面いっぱいに設けられたカウンター。天井やカウンター天板は、光沢のある仕上げで外部の風景を映しこむ。

Indirect lighting embedded within the ceiling naturally directs customers towards the interior.

天井には壁伝いに間接照明が埋め込まれ、利用者を奥へと自然に導いている。

A DESIGN ORIGINATING FROM A CONNECTION

A diamond-shaped pattern appears on the stainless steel mirror walls located at both ends of the corridor.

カウンターのあるスペースの両端は、メッシュ状のパターン加工を施したステンレスの鏡面壁となっている。

Run Pit by au Smart Sports

The locker and shower rooms are styled in masculine (top) and feminine tones (bottom). The spirit of the Palaceside Building, which was built in 1966, can be felt here through the stainless steel decorations and brick / marble decked interior.

ロッカーやシャワー設備のあるスペース。男性用（上）と女性用（下）。レンガや大理石などの部分は、1966年に建てられたパレスサイドビルの一部をそのまま残したもの。

A DESIGN ORIGINATING FROM A CONNECTION

INHABITANT STORE TOKYO

INHABITANT STORE TOKYO / 2009

Elements in Interrelationship

The INHABITANT STORE TOKYO is the lifestyle/sport brand's flagship store facing Harajuku's Cat Street. "Playfulness" and "Japanese-ness" are embodied in INHABITANT's freestyle expression of modern Japanese taste. This inspired us to envision a space thriving with the spontaneity of a casual stroll through the area known as "the back of Harajuku".
On each of the two floors, long plates cross diagonally the display areas with fitting rooms and counters positioned around it.
Artist Asao Tokolo elaborated tortoise-shell patterns that spread like clouds on the 2F ceiling. These icons, which fit with each other in any arrangement, can be found all over the store.
By capitalizing on the mutual relationship of the smaller units and through composition, we strived to create a space that would in turn blend in with the surrounding boutiques and residences.

相互に関係し合うエレメント

原宿・キャットストリートに面したライフスタイルスポーツブランド、INHABITANTの旗艦店。このブランドの自由で遊び心のある、現代的な日本の感覚を体現できるよう「遊び」と「和」をキーワードに、裏原宿の路上に迷い込んだかのような、偶発性を生み出す空間を考えた。
吹き抜けを介した1、2階が売場で、各階平面の対角に長いプレートが横断する。これを軸としてフィッティングルームや什器などを配している。
2階の天井面に広がる亀甲紋はアーティストの野老朝雄によるもので、どの辺を合わせてもつながっていく紋様が店内の全方位に展開している。
店舗や住居が雑多に集まる周囲の環境と連続させるため、小さなエレメントの集合が相互に関係を築きながら全体ができているような空間を目指した。

INHABITANT STORE TOKYO

Indirectly lit by lighting mounted on the ceiling plate, patterns on the 2F can be seen from the street. (p.146)

通りからの外観。2階のプレートに設けられた間接照明によって演出される天井の亀甲紋 (p.146)。

The long plate on the 1F can be used as a table to put articles on display and serve as a catwalk for special events. The plate's edge also becomes a step to the stairwell leading to the 2F.

1階の入口から吹き抜けの階段まで伸びるプレートは、商品のディスプレイ台、テーブル、イベント時のステージなどさまざまに機能する。プレートの端をステップに、壁から突き出している階段で2階に上がる。

A DESIGN ORIGINATING FROM A CONNECTION

INHABITANT STORE TOKYO

Looking down from the top of the stairs. All elements complement each other. (p.148)

階段吹き抜けを見下ろす。それぞれの要素が補完しあって機能する (p.148)。

The plate extending diagonally holds hanger racks on its under side. The interior of the stepped displays serve as fitting rooms. (top)

2階にもプレートが対角にまたがり、ハンガー什器として機能する。階段状のディスプレイ台の内部はフィッティングルームとなっている (上)。

The tortoise-shell pattern by Asao Tokolo is echoed on every face of this stool and again on the concrete floor. (bottom)

同じく野老朝雄による紋様を各面に展開したスツール。紋はコンクリートの床にも描かれている (下)。

A DESIGN ORIGINATING FROM A CONNECTION

EXHIBITION LIFE AND LIGHTING
くらしとあかり展 / 2007

The table top absorbs sunlight and glows in the dark at night, casting a shadow where objects once stood.
明かりのある状態（上）では天板が光を蓄え、夜になり暗くなると（下）、その蓄えられた光が発せられる。逆に物の置かれていた部分は影となる。

Shadows are like a memory of daylight that can be playfully swapped around.
物の影は、昼中の光が記憶されたように天板に残る（上）。実際の物と"記憶された影"を入れ替えて遊ぶ（下）。

The House-Watching Lights

The "Life and Lighting" exhibition organized by ENDO Lighting Corp. is a collaborative effort that brings architecture and lighting design together to redefine the concept of lighting.
For this project, we reflected on the nature of lighting and its relationship to both day and night times. The table and chair tops coated in luminous paint absorb sun rays during the day and glow in the dark at night, providing us with contrasting scenery between the times we leave and return home. Objects such as dishes or a flower vase cast a shadow against the glowing background, becoming one with the ambient darkness.
This was a proposal for lighting which welcomes the dweller back into his house.

留守番する光

遠藤照明が主催した、建築家と照明家による新しい明かりのあり方を提案する「くらしとあかり展」における展示計画。
ここでは、日中と夜間、両方に関係する明かりのあり方を考えた。蓄光塗料が塗られたテーブル面やイスの座面は、日中の太陽光を蓄え、帰宅時には真っ暗な部屋の中で発光する。それによってテーブルの上は、昼夜で見え方が反転する。モノの背景となっていたテーブル面や座面は、暗闇の中で発光し、その上に載っていた花瓶や、皿が置かれた部分は一転、暗闇と同化する影となって現れる。
帰宅時に主を迎え入れるような明かりを提案した。

A DESIGN ORIGINATING FROM A CONNECTION

EXHIBITION
"minä perhonen + torafu new / study"
ミナ ペルホネンとトラフの新作／習作 / 2009

hanger stool:
Pre-fabricated hangers, connected with each other by their hooks, are used in lieu of stool legs to symbolize minä perhonen as a fashion brand. The seating is decorated with the brand's line of fabrics.

ハンガー スツール
ミナ ペルホネンがファッションブランドであることからヒントを得た、ハンガーを用いたスツール。既製品のハンガーを三本脚に用い、フック部分を絡ませることで開き止めとしている。座面はミナ ペルホネンのテキスタイルで彩られる。

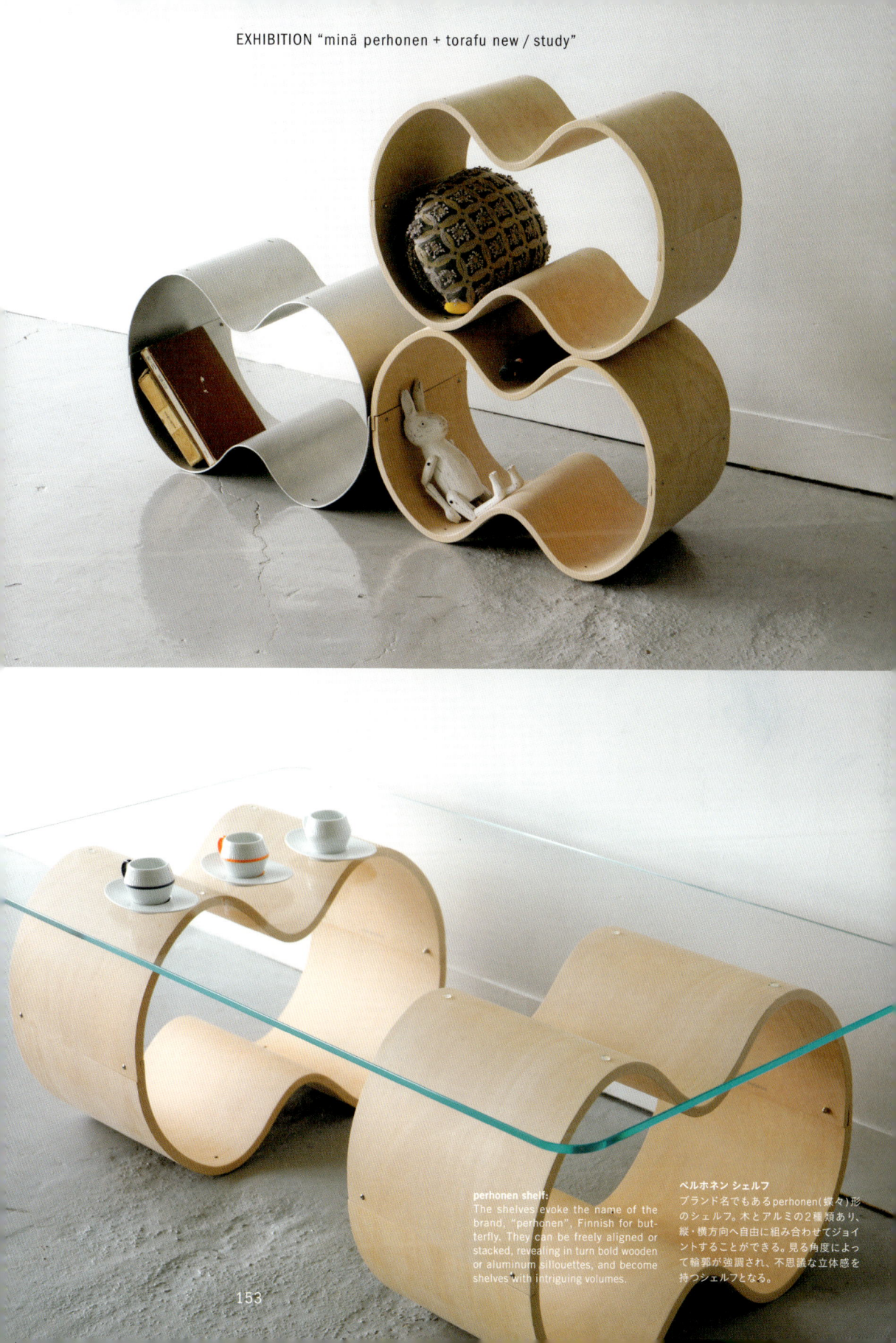

EXHIBITION "minä perhonen + torafu new / study"

perhonen shelf:
The shelves evoke the name of the brand, "perhonen", Finnish for butterfly. They can be freely aligned or stacked, revealing in turn bold wooden or aluminum sillouettes, and become shelves with intriguing volumes.

ペルホネン シェルフ
ブランド名でもあるperhonen(蝶々)形のシェルフ。木とアルミの2種類あり、縦・横方向へ自由に組み合わせてジョイントすることができる。見る角度によって輪郭が強調され、不思議な立体感を持つシェルフとなる。

A DESIGN ORIGINATING FROM A CONNECTION

Creating Furniture with minä perhonen

minä perhonen, an innovative fashion brand known for its fabrics weaved from various original ideas, presented its line of designer furniture at Hotel CLASKA's Gallery & Shop DO in December 2009. This collaborative effort inspired a bold lineup imbued with new values as we were given an opportunity to work on the designs of four out of the five types of furniture on display, namely the shelves, stools, rocking chairs and the sofa. All items feature fabrics by minä perhonen and elements from the world of fashion.
We aimed to propose furniture with new values that can be created in collaboration with minä perhonen.

ミナ ペルホネンと家具をつくる

さまざまなオリジナル図案によるファブリックで展開するファッションブランド、ミナ ペルホネンとのコラボレーション家具の展示・販売を、2009年12月にクラスカにあるGallery & Shop "DO" で開催。
発表された5点の家具のうち、シェルフ、スツール、ロッキングチェア、ソファのデザインに携わった。それぞれ、ミナ ペルホネンのファブリックを用いたり、ファッションで使われるツールなどを取り入れたりしている。
ミナ ペルホネンとの協働によって生み出される、新しい価値観を持った家具を提案した。

EXHIBITION "minä perhonen + torafu new / study"

Konpou sofa:
A customized wooden crate whose upper lid can be propped up to be used as a backrest, revealing a compartment of assorted minä perhonen cushions. A traveling sofa ready to be shipped halfway across the globe.

コンポウ ソファ
梱包用の木箱をカスタマイズしたソファ。ミナ ペルホネンのクッションが梱包された木箱を開け、フタを背もたれにし、クッションを並べるとソファへと姿を変える。そのまま輸送することのできる、旅するソファである。

A DESIGN ORIGINATING FROM A CONNECTION

CHELFITSCH "FREETIME"
チェルフィッチュ「フリータイム」/ 2008

CHELFITSCH "FREETIME"

Creating a New Horizon

We designed the set piece for the play *Freetime*, directed by Toshiki Okada and performed by the Chelfitsch company.

The action takes place in a family restaurant. We were not to completely recreate the setting, but only to suggest it on a superficial plane. Keeping in mind that an elaborate set could hamper the troupe's signature freeflowing movements, we were asked to create an abstract décor, prompting them to expand their corporeality by bringing the notion of set to a whole new level. The base plane is set at the imaginary height of 550mm above ground, and only the top parts of chairs and tables remain visible while the rest is buried beneath it. The chair and the table on which one usually sits and eats no longer retain their original function, but only their symbolisms remain.

Lending from this environment, the seemingly levitating actors are able to roam freely in a gentle, floating manner, bringing the surreal world of Freetime to life.

新しい地平面をつくる

岡田利規主宰の演劇ユニット、チェルフィッチュの新作公演「フリータイム」の舞台美術を手掛けた。舞台設定はファミレス。それを表面的に真似ても、完全に再現はできない。また、舞台設定に束縛されすぎると、劇団の特徴の一つでもある演者の多彩な動作を制限してしまう。舞台美術を背景以上の存在として、演者の動作に幅を持たせるきっかけになることを意識し、抽象化して実現することが求められた。地面から550mmという高さに仮想の平面を想定し、ファミレスのありふれたイスとテーブルのセットを切断する。切断された下半分は平面に埋もれ、高さが奪われたイスとテーブルは本来の機能を失って、その記号性だけが残る。

そこに立つだけで、演者が床からふわふわと浮かんで演じているような浮遊感のある光景は、人称が次々と入れ替わっていく「フリータイム」の独特な世界観を印象付ける。

What used to be tables and chairs, now only exists in its symbolism, reinterpreted through the actors' performances.

本来、イスとテーブルであった部分はその記号性だけが残り、演者の演技とともに別の意味を持ち始める。

Standing on this imaginary level, as if hovering over the floor, the actors are free to establish new relationships with a dining set that is removed from the conventional types of interactions.

演者はその上に立って床から浮いているような状態になることで、イスを引いて座ったり、テーブルで食事をとったりといった日常的な行為から解放される。

A DESIGN ORIGINATING FROM A CONNECTION

TABLE ON THE ROOF

テーブル オン ザ ルーフ / 2004

A 550mm High
Multi-purpose Surface

On the roof of the Hotel CLASKA there is nothing to interrupt our view. We were asked to design a new space which takes advantage of this great view. We were also asked to cover the concrete floor with a wooden decking as the space would be used for various events. However if we covered the entire ground with decking we would then need to heighten the existing handrail because of safety laws, and would then also need to consider appropriate outdoor tables and chairs.
Therefore our proposal was to make a huge table made of decking floating 550mm off the ground, set at a safe enough distance from the roof's edge to avoid adjusting the handrail. The table serves as a balcony floor, a chair and a stage.
The huge table plays with our perception and expectations in this unusual space, on the roof of the Hotel CLASKA.

550mmの高さががもたらす
多機能な平面

ホテル「クラスカ」の屋上に上がると視線をさえぎる建物もなく、遥か遠くまで見渡せる。その眺めの良さを活かして、さまざまなイベントに対応できる外部空間が求められた。
ウッドデッキ材を敷くことがアイデアとしてあったが、床全面にデッキを張ると、床面が少し上がって既存の手すりよりもさらに高い手すりが必要となってしまう。また別にテーブルやイスも必要となる。
そこで、外周からセットバックさせ、イスとテーブルの中間的な扱いとして床面から550mm浮かせた巨大な"テーブル"を提案した。このテーブルは、縁側のような床であり、イスであり、舞台でもある。
巨大なテーブルというアイデアが、既成のスケール感を狂わせ、非日常的なオン ザ ルーフ（屋上空間）を演出する。

TABLE ON THE ROOF

A big pergola extends from the entrance over the table like a green roof.

屋上エントランスと連続して、テーブルを横断する大きなパーゴラによって緑の屋根がかかる。

A DESIGN ORIGINATING FROM A CONNECTION

The table floating over concealed lighting at dusk.
間接照明で夕闇に浮いて見える巨大なテーブル。

The counter's legs are made of a series of raw cut Douglas-fir.
カウンターの脚は、切り出した無垢のベイマツ材を連結したもの。

TABLE ON THE ROOF

The exterior of Hotel CLASKA on Meguro Boulevard. (left)
目黒通り沿いに建つ、クラスカの外観 (左)。

Benches on the table were made of cork to gain water resistance and portability. (right)
コルクでつくられたテーブル上のベンチ。耐水性と持ち運びのしやすさを考慮した (右)。

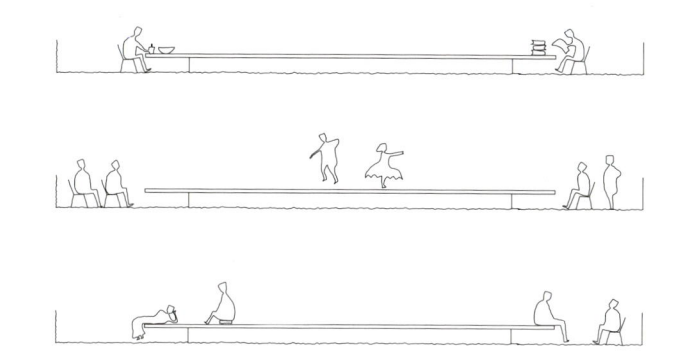

The roof before it was redesigned. There was nothing but a cooling tower.
施工前の屋上。冷却塔がある以外は何もなかった。

The joists support a table elevated 550mm from the floor level.
既存の床レベルから550mm浮かしたテーブルを支える根太。

161

A DESIGN ORIGINATING FROM A CONNECTION

Deck
デッキ / 2010

A Deck in Midair

This product was presented at the DESIGNEAST event held in Osaka during which a workshop invited visitors to assemble their purchased item. The ad-hoc deck outstretches like a small balcony in a crowded city. This deck is made out of a single plank of wood, when assembled, it is enough to easily hook onto a handrail as a small table. The deck will hold your drink in midair and seeds for your feathery friends.

空中のデッキ

大阪で開催されたイベント「DESIGNEAST」のために考案したプロダクト。イベント期間中のワークショップにおいて、購入した人がその場でつくって持ち帰ることができるよう求められた。
手すりから外に張り出したデッキ材を小さいテーブルのように使ってみることで、密集した都市の狭いバルコニーを少しだけ広げることを意図した。
この小さいテーブルは、1本のデッキ材から手すりに引っかかる分だけのわずかな材料でシンプルに組み上げられる。

6

TURNING THE MINIMUM INTO THE MAXIMUM

最小限を最大限に

The smallest cues, such as a slight change of viewpoint can have the greatest effect.

ちょっとだけ視点を変えるような小さいきっかけから大きい効果を生み出すこと。

TURNING THE MINIMUM INTO THE MAXIMUM

BOOLEAN
(Tokyo University Tetsumon Cafe)
ブーリアン（東京大学医学部教育研究棟 鉄門カフェ）/ 2007

Holes in the partition wall offer views on the surroundings while benches provide a spot to hang out.
パーティションに穿たれた穴は風景を切り取る窓となり、ベンチに穿たれた穴はその周囲に溜まりの場所をつくる。

BOOLEAN (Tokyo University Tetsumon Cafe)

A New Scenery Cut Out by Virtual Spheres

This is an interior design project for a cafe space adjacent to the University of Tokyo Faculty of Medicine Experimental Research Building entrance. The space only had a vending machine corner and was covered with hard materials, such as stone flooring and walls, and stainless sash windows. In order to offset the feeling of such hard materials, we used two L-shaped wooden objects placed in a different orientation to make a partition wall and a bench.
We imagined variously-sized spheres floating around in three-dimensional space, leaving holes in the partition wall and bench as they passed through.
Holes overlapping each other make the place feel more open as if there were floating spheres passing through the wall and ceiling while providing students with a new perspective from which to view everyday life.

仮想の球が切り取る新しい風景

東京大学の医学部教育研究棟エントランス脇の待合スペースにカフェコーナーを設けるプロジェクト。一角に自動販売機が置かれただけであった空間は、石張りの床、壁やステンレスのサッシなど、硬質な材料に覆われている。そこに、既存の床・壁からオフセットさせた木製の二つのL型オブジェクトを向きを変えて配置し、それぞれパーティションやベンチとなるよう計画した。
仮想のモデリング空間において、さまざまな大きさの球を家具の周囲に浮遊させるように、三次元的に配置する。宙に浮かんだ球が、パーティションやベンチと交錯した部分を抜き取っていく。
幾重にも重なって穿たれた穴は、壁や天井を突き抜けて球が存在するかのように空間に広がりを感じさせる。同時に、日常の風景を切り取り、非日常的な視点を与える。

TURNING THE MINIMUM INTO THE MAXIMUM

We used the suppleness and warmth of 30mm thick lauan wood to offset the hard materials in the flooring, walls and window sash.

穿たれた穴は新しい風景を生み出す。既存の壁や床、サッシなど硬質な素材に対し、柔らかさ、温かさを感じられる厚さ30mmのラワン材を用いた。

BOOLEAN (Tokyo University Tetsumon Cafe)

An exterior view of the standing partition. The partition is 3980mm high. There is also a bench installed on the exterior that is identical to the interior one.

外部より立ち上がったパーティションを見る。パーティションは高さ3980mm。外部にも内部と同様のベンチを設置。

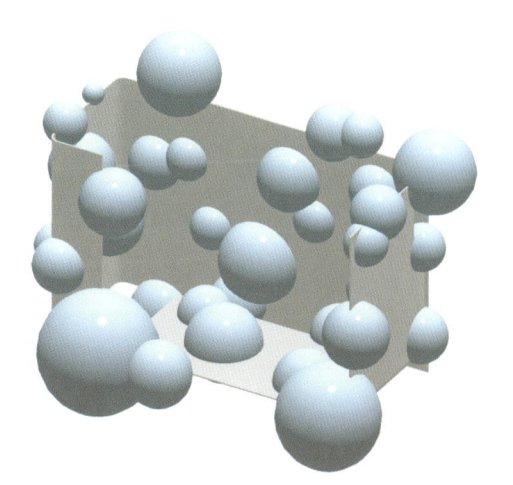

A model showing spheres of various sizes floating in the air.

宙に浮く大小さまざまな球のモデリング。

Partitions made at the workshop are assembled here on the spot.

工場で製作されたパーティションを現場で組み立てる。

TURNING THE MINIMUM INTO THE MAXIMUM

EXHIBITION "bones"
「骨」展 / 2009

When visitors look into the "Laboratory", they catch glimpses of various exhibiting pieces. Columns gently partition off each exhibit, inviting visitors to move about freely.

実験室では、林立する柱が会場全体に配置され、その柱の影に見え隠れしながら作品が置かれている。方向性を持たない柱は、作品の間を分節しながら、鑑賞者の自由な動きを誘発する。

A Scenery Baring Its Structural "Bones"

The site for 21_21 DESIGN SIGHT's exhibition "bones", directed by product designer Shunji Yamanaka, directs our attention to the relationship between function and form in industrial products, while considering the sophisticated structures of bones in living things.

The exhibition is comprised of a "Specimen Room" and a "Laboratory". The former possesses samples of "bones" of living things and industrial products while the latter introduces the works that were created to explore the "bones of the future."

The exhibition site is thickly forested with columns of three different sizes along with the existing concrete ones. As a structural element, it could be said that columns are the bones of a building. Columns seem to gain more freedom once they have been liberated from their primary function of upholding weight.

The subtle bony columns made with the bare minimum of materials required to maintain their shape, softly zone the large space. These columns also serve a supplementary function; providing a storage area for wires and other equipment. The fixtures and furnishing on which the pieces have been placed are also made of very minimal material.

空間の"骨"が風景をつくり出す

21_21 DESIGN SIGHTの企画展「骨」展の会場構成。プロダクトデザイナーの山中俊治をディレクターに迎え、生物の骨の洗練された構造を踏まえながら、工業製品の機能と形との関係に改めて目を向けていく展覧会である。

会場は、生物や工業製品の"骨"に目を向ける「標本室」と、"未来の骨"を探るために制作された作品を紹介する「実験室」の2パートで構成される。

会場には、コンクリートの柱に紛れるように3種のサイズの柱を林立させた。構造体としての柱は、建築物の骨と言える。しかし、本来の荷重を受ける機能から解放された柱は、より自由になる。

形態を保つ最小限の部材による文字通り骨だけの柱が、大きな空間を柔らかくゾーニングする。また機器の配線や設備を収納し、作品解説パネルのフレームにもなるなど補助的な役割を持つ。作品が置かれる什器も同様に、展示のための最小限の部材を残した形態をとる。

構造体から解放された骨が、機能的にさまざまな要請を受けながらも会場の風景をつくる存在となっていく。

TURNING THE MINIMUM INTO THE MAXIMUM

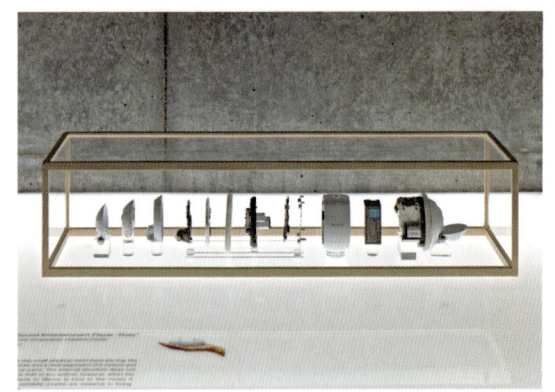

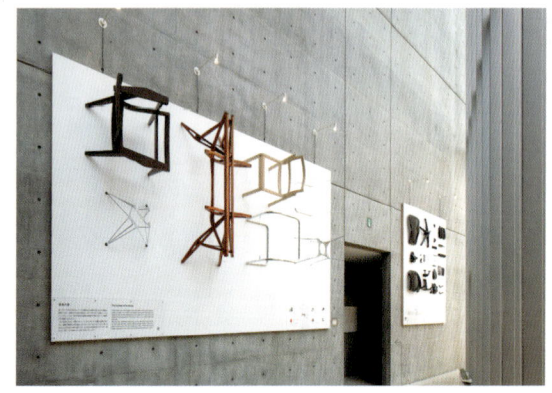

The 1F entrance. (top left)
1階のエントランス（左上）。

Relatively smaller objects such as precision apparatus are exhibited in a Z-shaped corridor. Contrary to usual flow planning, we located the Laboratory ahead of this narrow Specimen Room. (top right)
標本室では精密機器など小さめの展示が多いため、空間の狭さを活かしZ廊下と呼ばれる場所に展示した。その後に実験室が広がるよう、通常の動線とは逆の順路とした（右上）。

The display cases also respect the essence of the site. (bottom left)
展示ケースも実験室の柱と同様にフレームだけの形態をとる（左下）。

Wall exhibit of bones found in various furniture. (bottom right)
さまざまな家具の骨を見せる壁面展示（右下）。

EXHIBITION "bones"

Items currently under construction. The frames made of scaffolding and ladders are absorbed by a scenery of bone columns.

設営中の様子。仮設の足場や脚立などのフレームが柱の骨組みの風景に同化する。

TURNING THE MINIMUM INTO THE MAXIMUM

HOUSE IN INOKASHIRA

井の頭の住宅 / 2005

A Subtle Demarcation Line

We renovated a unit in a company house that was being fitted into a condominium. Looking at the bare dismantled concrete space, we decided to carefully minimize what we added to the room. By reducing as many obstructions as possible, we aimed to produce a space where the residents can feel the wind and the light, in tune with the changing seasons.
We drew a line which encircles and travels within the house in order to create a sense of being in one big room all the time.
The colorful inside surfaces of the furniture and art works displayed in every room were used to brighten up the quiet tone of the concrete.
We balanced with scrupulous care what to remodel and what to leave. We thought an unostentatious design could produce a space that would become a background of the residents' living and the furniture by making the most of the virtue the house had originally had.

繊細な境界線

元社宅の建物を、分譲マンションとして再生する計画の中で、1住戸のリノベーションを手掛けた。
解体された躯体のみの、ガランとした大きな一つの部屋のような状態に、住むために必要な最小限の要素だけを慎重に付け加えていくことにした。遮るものを少なくすることで、風が通り、光を感じ、四季の移ろいとともに生活できる空間を目指した。
大きな部屋の中にいることが感じられるよう、壁面の上下を塗り分けたラインを家の中全体に巡らせた。また、コンクリートなどの落ち着いたトーンの中で、鮮やかな色を持たせた家具の内側やアートが彩りを与える。
残す部分と新たに仕上げを施す部分とのバランスには細心の注意を払った。もともとの良さを活かし、主張しすぎないデザインにより、人や物の背景となるような空間を実現できると考えた。

HOUSE IN INOKASHIRA

We left the polka dots left by the plaster bonds after tearing the walls off. The one big room is mildly partitioned by the gray color painted on the cut ends of the wall openings. Lighting was improved by using concealed lights and blinds larger than the windows.

解体されてボードを剥がしたままの、水玉模様のようなボンド跡をあえて残している。躯体の壁と垂れ壁の小口面を濃いグレーで塗装し縁取ることで、ワンルームの空間をゆるやかに仕切っている。また、実際の開口よりも大きいブラインドと間接照明で壁面全体をより明るく感じられるようにした。

A room in a corporate housing building located near Inokashira Park. (left)

井の頭公園近くに建つもともと社宅として使われていた建物の一室（左）。

The excavated space. At a glance, both the client and we took to the stripped down room. (right)

発掘された空間。解体直後の状態を見て、クライアントも一目でその空間を気に入った（右）。

TURNING THE MINIMUM INTO THE MAXIMUM

RING PARKING
リング パーキング / 2006

A Pattern That Envelops Space

For this project we renovated the entrance of a condo cluttered with its residents' bicycles. We thought if we could use the vacant space next to the entrance as parking lots, it might add value to the condo.
The space had undergone heavy renovation a number of times and needed to be plastered. And since the pillars and the tie beams protrude from the walls, we planned to envelop the whole space with a homogeneous and symbolic pattern such as that of anti-slip rings. The rings are usually used for roads and would make parking lot users see this space as the extension of the road.
The space is filled with rings typically found on roads, and retains the extent of its directionality to become an extension of the road.

パターンで空間を包み込む

マンションのエントランス周りのリノベーション。もともと住民の自転車であふれていたことから、エントランス横の空きスペースを駐輪場とすることで、マンションに新しい価値がもたらされるように考えた。
このスペースは、何度もの改装を経て、壁面の凹凸が激しく、また柱型や梁型が目立つため、空間内を同じ左官仕上げで包み込む計画とした。そして空間を道路の延長ととらえられるように、滑り止めリングの記号性に注目し、左官仕上げのパターンとして採用した。
普段、床仕上げとして見慣れているリングに覆われた空間は、全方位的な広がりを持つと同時に、道路の延長のような場所として生まれ変わる。

The space beside the entrance which we remodeled was previously a vacant lot.
もともと空室であったエントランス横のスペースを改装した。

RING PARKING

The bare down-lights protruding from the ceiling are inspired by motorcycle headlights.

照明は、バイクのヘッドライトをイメージし、通常は天井に埋め込むダウンライトをむき出しで使用している。

The residents' bicycles cluttered the entrance, so we opted to secure a parking lot to preserve its function as a lobby. (top left)

もともとのエントランス周りは、住民の自転車であふれてしまい、玄関としての機能を損ねていたため、駐輪場の確保を優先した（左上）。

The homogeneous pattern is made by "vacuous ring method." Rings made of standardized solid rubber are pressed on the mortar at regular intervals with a jig. (right)

「真空リング工法」による型押し作業は、規格化されている硬質ゴム製のリングを、規定のピッチに切り欠いたジグにあてがってモルタル面に押し付けていく（右）。

KIRIKO BOTTLE

キリコ ボトル / 2007

Small Changes in a Familiar Sight

"Edo Design", an exhibition project by designers promoting the revival of artisans and tools in Japanese traditional craftsmanship and the spirit that has been handed down since the Edo period. Kiriko Bottle was made in collaboration with Tadayuki Okubo, a cut glass artisan, giving a new perspective from which to look at familiar glass bottles, utilizing conventional glass cutting techniques now considered quaint.
A soy sauce pot with a fish scale pattern around the neck, a milk bottle engraved with a tilted liquid level or a cow skin pattern created utilizing a special cutting technique, a wine bottle with a spiral pattern spreading from neck to bottom, a spice bottle with a hole for drawing divinatory sticks – things that are seen every day in the dining room were given a second life by the artistic craftsmanship of cut glass. Such small changes in a familiar sight enrich our lives.

日常を変えるささいな変化

江戸の伝統技術と心意気を現代に継承する名工と道具たちを、日常生活のシーンに復活させようとデザイナーが取り組むプロジェクト「江戸意匠」。
江戸切子師の大久保忠幸との合作となる「キリコ ボトル」は、記号のようになってしまった切子技術を普段見慣れた空きビンへ施すことによって、それぞれへの新たな眼差しを提供する。
魚のうろこ模様を首周りに施された醤油ビン、ボトルを傾けたときの液体の軌跡や特殊な加工で牛柄をまとった牛乳ビン、キャップのネジ切り溝が全体に螺旋模様を描いたワインボトル、中ぶたの穴を使っておみくじに生まれ変わった七味ビン。食卓のレギュラーたちが、江戸切子の技術によって生まれ変わる。そのささいな卓上の変化が日常の生活を豊かにする。

CMYK

CMYK / 2008

A Colorful Impression of Movement

We were approached to design a futsal ball as part of Italian furniture brand MAGIS Japan's PR campaign. A typical soccer ball consists of 12 black pentagonal faces and 20 white hexagonal faces assembled to give it the characteristic shape that can also be described as a "spherical truncated icosahedron". We decided to bring our own touch to the traditional black and white ball and revamp its design for the occasion.

By combining Cyan (C), Magenta (M) and Yellow (Y) in equal parts, we obtain Black, or Key (K), as it is known in the printing business. To illustrate this principle, we designed a ball that looks as if the colored pentagons have shifted from the impact of a kick.

The 7 colors obtained by the CMY combinations create a colorful impression of movement on the white background even when the futsal ball is at rest.

色のずれから生まれる動きのイメージ

家具ブランドMAGIS JapanのPR用に、フットサルボールのデザインを手掛けた。一般的にサッカーボールとしてイメージされているのは、黒い五角形のパネル12枚と白い六角形のパネル20枚で構成された形状(切頂二十面体)である。この白黒のボールに少し手を加えて、いつもとは違う視点を提供できればと考えた。

印刷上では、シアン(C)、マゼンタ(M)、イエロー(Y)を同比で混ぜると、黒(K)ができる。この原理を使い、あたかもボールを蹴った勢いで五角形のパターンがずれてしまったようなデザインとした。CMYの組み合わせから、白地に合計7色のカラフルな表情を持つことになる。

静止していても像がぶれているような、動的なイメージを持つフットサルボールができあがった。

TURNING THE MINIMUM INTO THE MAXIMUM

tapehook
tapehook / 2011

The tapehook can be used to hang small accessories or keys to add a decorative touch to your room.
テープフックを貼り、アクセサリーやカギを引っ掛ければ、部屋に彩りを与えることができる。

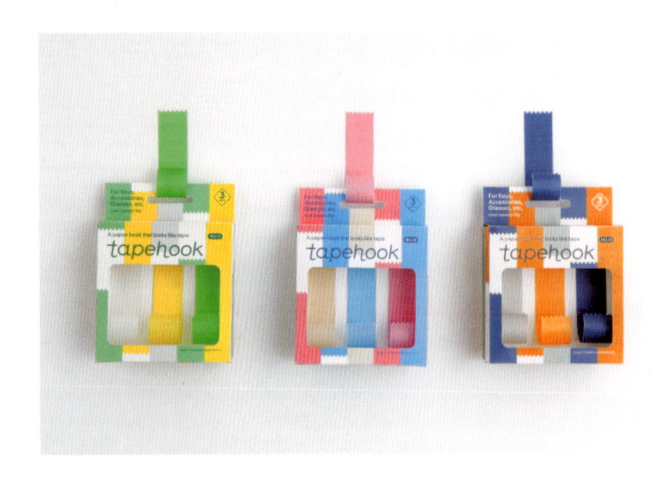

The packaging reveals the tape-like shape and its purpose at a glance. There are three differently colored hooks per box.
テープの形状と用途が一目で分かるパッケージ。1箱3色各1枚入り。

· tapehook

A Paper Hook That Looks Like Tape

This product was created for the "Kami no Dougu" (Paper Tools) exhibition held by the "Kami no Kousakujo", a project advanced by designers and print processing plants who seek to explore the potential of tools manufactured from processed paper. Taking hints from the unique characteristics of tape, the paper hook was proposed under the theme "Products that take advantage of adhesive techniques". Curling the tip like a piece of tape, the hook is soaked then dried. This process gives it enough strength to hang small accessories or keys. Looking like cut-out tape, this paper hook creates a sense of wonder, and the unpredictable resilience its appearance defies gives it an extraordinary presence.

テープのような紙のフック

デザイナーと印刷加工所が紙を加工してできる道具の可能性を追求するプロジェクト「かみの工作所」による展覧会「かみの道具」のために製作されたプロダクト。テーマである「粘着の技術を活かしたプロダクト」に対し、テープの特性からヒントを得た紙のフックを提案した。
テープの巻きぐせのように紙を丸め、形を固定して水に浸し乾燥させることで、アクセサリーやカギなどが引っ掛かる強度を持たせた。
テープを切った形がそのままフックになるという面白さと、見た目よりも強度があるという意外性が不思議な存在感を与えている。

TURNING THE MINIMUM INTO THE MAXIMUM

airvase
空気の器 / 2010

A Paper Bowl That Envelops Air

This product was created for the "Kami no Dougu" (Paper Tools) exhibition held by the "Kami no Kousakujo" project. Each designer was assigned a color under the theme "Taking advantage of the characteristics of spot colors". Torafu was assigned the color green so we proposed a paper bowl that blends yellow and blue to obtain green.
This paper bowl envelops air so you can freely change its shape by spreading and molding it. While paper makes it thin and lightweight, it can also be strong and resistant when shaped like a bowl. The colors on each side of the paper create a different impression depending on the angle at which it is viewed.

空気をはらんだ紙の器

「かみの工作所」による展覧会「かみの道具」のためのプロダクト。「特色を活かしたプロダクト」というテーマの中、各デザイナーそれぞれに色が与えられた。トラフに与えられたカラーは緑色で、それに対し、黄色と青色の混じり合いによって緑色を表現した紙の器を提案した。
空気を包みこむように形を自由に変えられる紙の器は、広げ方によって、自由な形をつくることができる。紙でできているため薄くて軽いが、器になると張りと強度が出る。紙の表と裏で色が異なるため、見え方によって印象の変わる不思議な器。

By expanding a sheet of paper into a volume, it becomes a bowl in its own right.
1枚の紙から立体的に広げていくと、自立する器になる。

airvase

It can be shaped into various forms and freely used for any purpose, such as making a tray for small objects, a flower vase decoration or to gift-wrap a wine bottle.

広げ方によっていろいろな形ができる。小物を入れるトレイ、花瓶の装飾、ワインのギフト包装など、使い方は自由。

A group of three sheets form one package. The three combinations are yellow and blue, pink and beige, and white. There are also limited editions and new designs for sale.

1セット3枚入りのパッケージ。最初のイエロー×ブルーに続き、ピンク×ベージュ、ホワイト、そのほか限定販売のものや、新作も発売。

TURNING THE MINIMUM INTO THE MAXIMUM

airvase

Each work was printed according to the drawn blueprint. We did studies by carefully cutting each one by hand so as not to cut the mesh. As many as 30 test pieces were produced while taking into consideration the size, shape of cut, and spacing of each.
図面を描いて印刷し、網目が切れないように一つずつ手で切り、大きさや切り込みの形状と間隔を検討しながら30個ほど試作した。

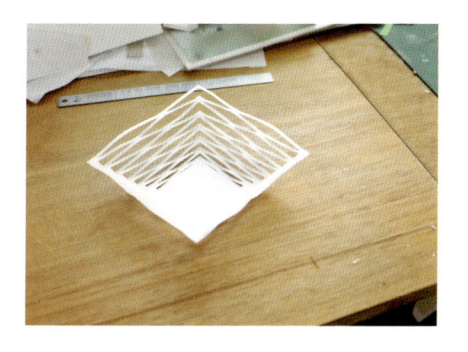

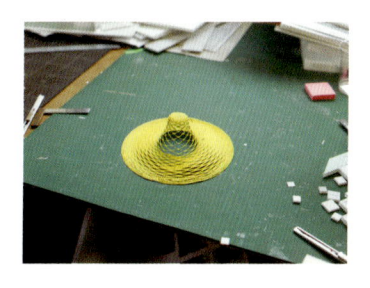

The bowls display a variety of expressions depending on their color, pattern or usage. (p.182)
色や柄、または使い方によってさまざまな表情を見せる空気の器。(p.182)。

TURNING THE MINIMUM INTO THE MAXIMUM

The exhibition held at Spiral Garden in Aoyama. 600 airvases, displayed with various patterns or fluttering in the air above, create a delicate scenery.
青山のスパイラルで行われた展覧会の様子。600個の空気の器で見せる、柄のバリエーションと宙にゆらめく繊細な光景。

TORAFU AND TOKYO
トラフと東京

COLUMN 03

AKIHABARA
秋葉原

HARAJUKU
原宿

AROUND THE IMPERIAL PALACE
皇居周辺

MEGURO
目黒

① NIKE 1LOVE (2007.01–2008.01)
② GREGORY TOKYO STORE
③ INHABITANT STORE TOKYO
④ 3M store (2010.08–12)
⑤ HermanMiller Store Tokyo
⑥ Run Pit by au Smart Sports
⑦ TORANOANA AKIHABARA (2006.07–2009.07)
⑧ TEMPLATE IN CLASKA & TABLE ON THE ROOF
⑨ HOUSE IN OOKAYAMA
⑩ NIKE PRESSROOM
⑪ minä perhonen arkistot
⑫ NIKE JMC
⑬ KAYAC Ebisu Office
⑭ DWJ Office
⑮ BOOLEAN (Tokyo University Tetsumon Cafe)

Torafu's office is located in a residential part of Tokyo. Torafu, which has many design outlets, confronts Tokyo's uniquely powerful commercial and urban environments, and undertakes the design of many shops and exhibitions.

Torafu is intimately familiar with the popularly named "Cat Street" in Harajuku since they designed three shops found together on this street – NIKE 1LOVE (①, p.104), GREGORY TOKYO STORE (②, p.102), and INHABITANT STORE TOKYO (③, p.146).
Fashion stores catering to the youth are what primarily line the sidewalks of this quaint pedestrian road on a blind ditch in a residential area. Always conscious of this townscape that is like a careless accumulation of volumes and materials, Torafu skillfully constructs their designs.
At GREGORY TOKYO STORE, a mixed-element image connected to the design which features diverse mountain climbing motifs. INHABITANT STORE TOKYO capitalizes on the experience of discovery that can be found on the streets by applying this to the visual sequence. And at the nearby Omotesando 3M store (④, p.96), it almost appears as if the tile patterns of the pavement are connected to the glass storefront. People are able to feel these material textures as it switches to chemical products, drawing them into the world of 3M.

トラフは東京の住宅街に事務所がある。
いろいろなデザインへの適応力を発揮するトラフは、東京独自のパワフルなコマーシャルや都市環境とも向き合い、ショップや展示のデザインも多く手掛けている。

原宿にある通称「キャットストリート」は、トラフにとって結果的に馴染みの深い通りとなった。
「NIKE 1LOVE」（①、p.104）、「GREGORY TOKYO STORE」（②、p.102）、「INHABITANT STORE TOKYO」（③、p.146）と連鎖するように三つのショップを手掛けている。本来は住宅街にある暗渠上の遊歩道で、現在は若者向けのファッションストアなどが建ち並ぶ。そのボリュームも素材感も無造作に積み重ねていったような街並みを意識しながら、巧みにデザインを構築している。
GREGORY TOKYO STOREでは、要素が混在するイメージから多彩な登山のモチーフをちりばめたデザインにつながっている。INHABITANT STORE TOKYOもさまざまな発見のできる通りの体験が、店舗内部のシークエンスにもそのまま運用されている。それらからほど近い表参道の「3M store」（④、p.96）では、舗道のタイルパターンがそのままガラス張りの店内とつながっていくようなイメージで考えられている。素材感だけがケミカルな製品に切り替わり、3Mの世界観に引き込まれる。

COLUMN 03

HARAJUKU 原宿

Many young people gather around Harajuku where an eclectic collection of shops converge at the intersection of Omotesando and Meiji Dori Avenue.
多くの若者で賑わう原宿界隈は、表参道と交差する明治通りを中心に多彩なショップ群が建ち並ぶ。

AROUND THE IMPERIAL PALACE 皇居周辺

The places surrounding the Imperial Palace are perfectly maintained like a park, making it a recreation area for people. The adjacent Marunouchi district is fraught with offices, and appears like an extension of those comforting places.
皇居周辺は公園のように整備がなされ、人々の憩いの場となっている。隣接する丸の内地区はその心地よさを延長したような通りのたたずまいを持つオフィス街だ。

The beautiful cityscape that is preserved in the vicinity of the Imperial Palace is like an exception that stands in contrast to the somewhat chaotic charm of Tokyo. The roads with their greenery and sense of wide-open space make for a pleasant walking experience.
The HermanMiller Store Tokyo (⑤, p.64), located in Marunouchi, was designed as though it were a part of nature, and as an extension of the context of its surroundings. By providing a design that abstractly resembles trees and sunlight filtering through tree tops that accomodates for flexible activities just like in a park, the store manages to infuse the interior with the kind of pleasant sensations experienced in the surrounding area.
Run Pit by au Smart Sports (⑥, p.140) directly incorporates the Imperial Palace moat as a function of its building. The focus here is not on the interior, but rather on how effectively it serves as a device to extend the city's functionality as a running course.

Speaking of chaotic Tokyo, Torafu also does work in the already world-famous district of Akihabara. TORANOANA AKIHABARA (⑦, p.78) is representative of a true Akihabara-type shop. The many enthusiasts who visit this shop are not so much interested in the interior design but rather in the products themselves. Akihabara's image is that of a high-density district that is like a flood of information, and this image has been incorporated into the store with white vapor-like appliances and interiors.

皇居周辺は、カオスな魅力があるととらえられる東京でも例外的に美しい街並みが維持されている。緑化整備された道路や広々としたスケール感など、歩いているのが苦にならない。
丸の内にある「ハーマンミラーストア東京」（⑤、p.64）では、そのコンテクストの延長上で、店舗が自然に存在するようにつくられている。木々や木漏れ日を抽象化したデザインや、公園のように柔軟なアクティビティーを提供することで、周辺の体験の気持ちよさを店舗に引き込んでいる。
さらに、「Run Pit by au Smart Sports」（⑥、p.140）ではその施設の機能から、もっと直接的に皇居のお堀を取り込んでいる。インテリアを設えるというよりも、ランニングコースとして街の機能を拡張する、その装置としていかに働くかを主眼としている。

逆に東京のカオスといえば、もはや世界的に有名な秋葉原でもトラフは仕事をしている。「とらのあな AKIHABARA」（⑦、p.78）は、"アキバ"なショップの代表的存在だが、ここを訪れる多くのマニアにとっての関心は、過剰なインテリアのデザインではなく、そこに置かれる商品そのものだ。情報の洪水のような高密度な街のイメージが、そのまま持ち込まれ、モノとしての什器やインテリアは白く気化してしまっているようである。

AKIHABARA 秋葉原

A city unlike anywhere else in the world, submerged by the sheer amount of products and culture that are particular to Japan. This place attracts tourists from all over the country as well as abroad.

世界でも例のない日本独自のカルチャーとプロダクトが膨大な量をもって街を埋め尽くす。日本中はもちろん、海外からの観光客も多く訪れる。

MEGURO 目黒

Meguro Chuo-Cho is close to Gakugei Daigaku Station on the Toyoko line. This is where it all began for Torafu. The CLASKA is found alongside many furniture stores on Meguro Avenue, also known as "Furniture Street".

東横線・学芸大学駅からほど近い目黒・中央町界隈。トラフのすべてはここから始まった。クラスカの建つ目黒通りは多くの家具ショップなどが並び、家具ストリートとして知られる。

Meguro – Chuocho, a residential area slightly removed from the downtown core, is a district full of memories for Torafu. Hotel CLASKA is located here. This is where Torafu's first work, TEMPLATE IN CLASKA (⑧, p.14), was created. Moreover, Torafu's first office was a rented space in the CLASKA building. They also undertook TABLE ON THE ROOF (⑧, p.158) here. Torafu was stimulated by the hotel environment, which represents an extraordinary meeting place for a diversity of people from around the world. The changing activities and ways in which the facilities were used were some of the many aspects that would prove to be useful in creating future designs.

The TEMPLATE IN CLASKA serves as the benchmark for Torafu's designs. Not only was it their first work, but Torafu were greatly perplexed by the balance between the abstract and concrete elements of the design since they worried what the powerfully-shaped wall might impose on the small room. As an architectural consideration, the idea to not leave behind any inadvertent lines remained until the end.

The favorable remarks they received for the completed works made Torafu realize once again that it was not enough to simply stop at a design that filled the requirements. Stirring people's emotions was also an important function, and objects found within the scenery were also a part of the design.

トラフにとって思い出の街は、目黒・中央町という都心からは少し離れた住宅街だ。ここにはホテル「クラスカ」がある。彼らの最初の作品でもある「テンプレート イン クラスカ」（⑧、p.14）が生まれた場所であり、最初の事務所もクラスカ内に借りた。続けて「テーブル オン ザ ルーフ」（⑧、p.158）も手掛けた。ホテルという、国籍を問わず多彩な人の流れがある非日常的な場所で、さまざまな刺激を受けたという。アクティビティーの変化や各施設の使われ方など、のちの設計に役立った部分も多いはずだ。

そして「テンプレート イン クラスカ」は、トラフのデザインのベンチマークともなっている。小さい部屋における強いカタチの壁面が押し付けにならないか。単に初めての仕事という以上に、デザインの抽象と具象のバランスに対して、非常に迷ったという。建築的な思考として、不用意な線は残したくない、という思いは最後まで残った。結果、できあがった作品への評価から、要件を満たすだけの設計に留まるのではなく、人の感情を動かすことも大事な機能であり、物も含めた風景というものもデザインなんだ、ということに改めて気付いたという。

TORAFU ARCHITECTS IDEA + PROCESS 2004-2011

189

[Intent]-[Author]=[Story]

Jun Aoki

On the same day, Torafu showed me two homes they had designed named House in Kohoku and House in Ookayama. The former, intended as a small pied-à-terre for a couple absent for long periods at a time, is found in a hilly residential area next to Shin-Yokohama Station. The latter is located in a residential area near the heart of Tokyo where two generations cohabit and tries to make the best use of the land available. Their radically different inception and execution produced two radically different houses where there are plenty of common features to be found as they are both Torafu homes.

The first striking resemblance is the lack of fastidiousness of their construction. The basic form of the House in Kohoku is a regular quadrilateral composed of four concrete columns shaped like acorn barnacles. Stuck to its sides are two separate lumps that are the entranceway and the storage area. The irregular shape of the house seems to follow an internal logic rather than a ground schematization. We are left with the impression of a concrete island that fell from space and landed by chance in the middle of Kohoku. An uncontrived construction like a building alien to the ground on which it stands. In contrast, the House in Ookayama is a rectangular solid whose right-angles and simple elongated layout matches the long strip of land on which it stands (in fact, the roof had to be obliquely cut off in two directions due to setback restrictions but nonetheless appears as a rectangular solid when viewed from the street). The building closely matches the plot but is separated from the site boundaries by a narrow aisle of broken stones surrounding the core of the building. To gain access to the house, one must engage in the aisle and enter through a door on the right-hand side. The entrance, bearing no resemblance to a vestibule, feels as if the entrance itself was meant to be there in the first place, but nobody quite figured out how. The eaves above, which might well seem as if extemporaneously prepared, reinforces this feeling. Even where one would expect concrete to be laid, we find a broken stone approach, which brings us to the conclusion that even the house we had considered at first glance to be rooted in its plot, was in fact built as if it had landed there from outer space.

However, this type of uncontrived construction could not have come to be if it were truly disconnected from its base. A type of construction completely devoid of fastidiousness that is finely attuned to its surroundings, yet tries to negate this by pushing the envelope to the furthest extent possible. "A finely honed absence of fastidiousness", this unusual word combination summarizes the ambivalence that exists between the deliberate and random aspects of the House in Ookayama.

Incidentally, we begin to realize that the House in Kohoku isn't free of fastidiousness as we had first imagined. The hilly landscape facing north prevents sun rays from reaching the house while adjacent rows of houses accentuate the darkness. Unless the site is very large, it will remain humid and dark no matter how far north the house is settled. It was decided instead to leave as much room between it and the other houses in order to increase air flow. The objective was to keep the construction as small as possible in the center of the site by itself. An arrangement grounded in logic whose intentions are astutely camouflaged to give the impression that it was randomly put there. The shape of the house is also the conclusion of a logical process itself– providing natural lighting, and deterring crime during prolonged absences– masked by the use of the impersonal concrete material. This is an important part of the design where, once again, we are made privy to the ambivalence that exists between the deliberate and random aspects of the house.

TEXT BY JUN AOKI

The bolder the intent, the more discreet the execution.

This statement doesn't only apply to architecture and has in fact become one of Torafu's most remarkable features in many works. Let's take for example the "Yokoyama Yuichi – A complete record of Neo Manga" exhibition. Here the artist's world was transposed onto a track-and-field narrative where a semi-directive line of flow makes visitors move around the track. The site was, in fact, loaded with artificiality, but they nonetheless succeeded in creating an immersive experience without communicating this impression to the visitor, and I truly admire that.

They achieved this because the exhibition site naturally lent itself to the shape of a running track. Upon entering the site we can see that the furthermost wall is curved. By following the glass presentation cases fixed along the track, we are making laps without even noticing. We soon find ourselves caught in a circular motion along the track.

Two concentric tracks nonchalantly placed at the center of the unmodified surroundings. Far from feeling out of place, they are in fact logically derived from the world of Yokoyama Yuichi and the shape of the site, and included many thought-out details. Nonetheless, they used coarse materials such as veneer, which set their work loose and concealed with dexterity the high degree of intent behind the execution. In this light, we begin to appreciate the resemblance with their treatment of the House in Kohoku.

Trying to hide the intent ultimately serves to hide the author. By removing the author from the equation we are left with a story– an anonymous story– where all the actors involved are bound by a clear, common and specific story line.

Consequently, [Intent] – [Author] = [Story] can be expressed as [Intent] = [Story] + [Author]. This can be interpreted as "the intent, is a story belonging to the collective as appropriated by an individual". Indeed, every story needs a storyteller: an author. But an author who fails to detach himself from his work would eventually drive away his audience and the same goes for a designer whose stylish designs cannot be enjoyed at ease.

Luckily, this is the exact opposite of what Torafu strives to accomplish. By removing themselves from the equation, they invite others into an open book while preserving the story's impact. They expand and loosen this space up for others to come into, and this is where the power of Torafu's design resides. Their conception of design can be summed up in "a finely honed absence of fastidiousness". Standing in front of one of their designs, we offer no opposition as it seeps right into us, but before we even realize this, their story has already entered our subconscious.

I first came to this realization when I noticed a piece of garden oddly standing out in a north-western corner of the House in Kohoku site and unexpectedly saw vegetables being cultivated there.

Jun Aoki

Born in 1956, Yokohama. Having graduated from the University of Tokyo (1982), Aoki joined Arata Isozaki & Associates (1983–1990) before establishing his own practice in 1991. His accomplishments span a wide range of residential, public as well as commercial buildings. Aoki received the Minister of Culture's Prize for the Promotion of the Arts in 2004. Representative works include "Mamihara Bridge", "S", "Gata Museum", "Louis Vuitton Omotesando Store" and "Aomori Prefectural Museum of Arts".

〈作為〉−〈作者〉=〈ストーリー〉

青木 淳

トラフが設計した住宅を二つ、同じ日に見せてもらった。「港北の住宅」と「大岡山の住宅」。一方の「港北の住宅」は、新横浜駅にほど近い丘陵地帯の住宅地にあって、長期不在が多いご夫婦が住まわれるための小さな家で、もう一方の「大岡山の住宅」は、東京の都心に近い住宅地にある、2世帯のための、土地を目一杯に利用しつくした家だ。成り立ちがまるで違う。だから、できあがった家もすごく違う。と言っても、両方ともトラフが設計した住宅であるわけで、共通点も、もちろん、いっぱいある。

共通することのなかで、まず目についたのは、建ち方が無造作なこと。「港北の住宅」は、四つのフジツボみたいな形が寄り集まって正方形を成しているのが基本形で、そこに玄関の塊と納戸の塊の二つの塊が、それぞれ別の辺にくっついて、いびつになっている。その形は、土地の形から、割り出されたというより、内からのロジックで出てきたよう。だからか、コンクリートの塊が、宇宙から落ちてきて、ここにたまたまポンと着地した、というような印象を受ける。土地に無関心な建物、あるいは、無造作な建ち方。

それに対して、「大岡山の住宅」は、いたってシンプルな形で、土地が細長い長方形の形なら、建物も薄い直方体（実は、斜線制限のせいで、頂部が2方向に削られているのだけれど、道からは直方体に見える）。建物がすっぽりと土地にはまっている。そして、その建物と敷地境界との間の隙間に、細かい砕石が敷かれている。家に入るためには、その隙間に入っていく。すると、右手にドアがある。それが入口。ぜんぜん「玄関」らしくない。まるで、「入口」は計画に入っていたけれど、「そこへ至るアプローチ」の方は入っていなかった、という感じ。間に合わせでつけたとも見える庇がその感を強めている。せめてコンクリートを打ったらと思うのに、アプローチもやっぱり砕石のまま。そう、一見、土地から割り出されたと思えるこの住宅もまた、結局は、土地に無関心な、宇宙から落ちてきた建物としてつくられているのだ。

しかし、こういう種類の無造作は、ほんとうに土地に無関心であったら生まれない。それは、その場所に敏感に呼応してつくっておきながら、その作為を打ち消す方向に、それ以外のものではありえないというところまで追い込んでできた種類の、一分のくるいもない無造作なのだ。一分のくるいもない、研ぎ澄まされた無造作、というのは、なんだか変な言葉づかいだけれど。ともかく、「大岡山の住宅」には、作為と無作為の、そんなアンビバレンツがある。

そのことに気づけば、「港北の住宅」もまた、その建ち方がけっして無造作でないことがわかってくる。北に向かって大きく雛壇状に下っていく土地では、その土地の高低によってだけでもう日射が遮られる。そこに家が建ち並ぶわけだから、さらに暗くなる。よほど大きな敷地でないかぎり、建物をどんなに北に寄せても、日当たりは悪く、じめじめとしやすいことにはかわりない。だから、無理して北に寄せず、むしろ北側も含め、できるかぎりまわりの家からゆったり距離をとって、風通しをよくする。つまり、敷地のほぼ中央に、ぽつんと、できることなら、こぢんまりと小さく建てる。この住宅の配置計画は、実は、とても論理的なのだ。にもかかわらず、その作為を明示せず、逆に無作為に置かれたように思わせるようにできている。家そのものの形にしたって、長期に及ぶ外出中の防犯と採光を考えれば、それはそれでひとつのきれいな論理的帰結だ。でもここでも、その作為が、無愛想なコンクリート打ち放しという仕上げによって、打ち消されている。その結果としての無造作。それが、ここでのデザインの力点になっている。やっぱり、作為と無作為のアンビバレンツがある。

強い作為でありながら、その作為性は打ち消される。

なにも建築に限らない。それは、トラフの多くの仕事に見られる大きな特徴だ。たとえば、「横山裕一 ネオ漫画の全記

録」は、アーティスト・横山裕一の世界が「陸上トラック」というストーリーに置き換えられたものであったけれど、これなどは、そのトラックに沿って、観客が半強制的に周回させられ、その観客の運動もまた含めて「陸上トラック」＝横山裕一の世界になってしまうという、すさまじいまでの作為に満ちた会場構成だった。なのに、その作為が、観客に「やらされている」という感覚を与えることがまるでない。そこがすごいところだ。

なぜ、そんなことになるのか、と言えば、この展示室自体の奥のコーナーが丸くなっていて、もともとのその空間を「陸上トラック」と見立てたことが、ごく自然だったからだ。展示室に入る。最初に目につくのが、もともとの奥の壁の湾曲。そしてそれに誘われて、壁に沿ってガラスケースのなかの展示をひとつひとつ見ていく。知らないうちに周回している。ぼくたちは、そして、いつの間にか、トラックに沿っての周回運動に引き込まれてしまっている。

まわりはもともとのままで、その中央に二重のトラック台が、無造作に、ポンと置かれている。しかし、そのトラックはけっして場違いなものではなく、この展示室の形と横山裕一の世界から、論理的に導き出されてきたもの。しかも、よく練られたディテールでできている。にもかかわらず、ベニヤというざっくばらんな素材の使用。それで、スキができる。作為性が消えてしまう。こうして見れば、「港北の住宅」と、この会場構成はとても似ている。

なぜ作為性が打ち消されるかと言えば、その作為の背後にいるはずの作者の姿を消すためだ。作為から作者を引けば、ストーリーが残る。ストーリーは、特定の誰かのものでもない。それに関わるみんなが共有するある特定の明確な方向性、それがストーリーだ。

〈作為〉－〈作者〉＝〈ストーリー〉。式を変形して、〈作為〉＝〈ストーリー〉＋〈作者〉。「作為とはみんなのものであるはずのストーリーを個人が専有したもの」と読める。たしかに、まずは誰かが語ろうとしなければ、ストーリーは生まれない。作者は必要。でも、それをいつまでも自分だけのものにしようとすれば、そのデザインは人を拒絶する。かっこいいデザイン。だけど、ちっともリラックスできない。

トラフがやろうとしているのは、ちょうどその逆のことだ。つくったストーリーから自分を消そうとする。ストーリーの強度は保つけれど、閉じたストーリーを開いて、人を招きいれる。人が入り込める余地を、ひっぱってぎゅーっと、拡げる。つまり、スキをつくる。そのことに、すべてのデザイン力がつぎ込まれている。「研ぎ澄まされた無造作」。それがトラフにとってのデザインの意味だ。トラフがデザインしたものには、身構えることなく、スッと入っていける。いや、そう思う前に、無意識に、そのストーリーに入り込んでしまっている。

「港北の住宅」の敷地の北西の角には、変に余ってしまっているような小さな庭がある。そこで思いがけず、野菜が栽培されているのを見て、ぼくはそう思った。

青木 淳

1956年横浜生まれ。82年東京大学大学院修了。83-90年磯崎新アトリエに勤務後、91年青木淳建築計画事務所設立。個人住宅、公共建築から商業建築まで多方面で活躍。2004年度芸術選奨文部科学大臣新人賞受賞。代表作に、「馬見原橋」、「S」、「潟博物館」、「ルイ・ヴィトン 表参道店」、「青森県立美術館」等。

P.14 TEMPLATE IN CLASKA
テンプレート イン クラスカ

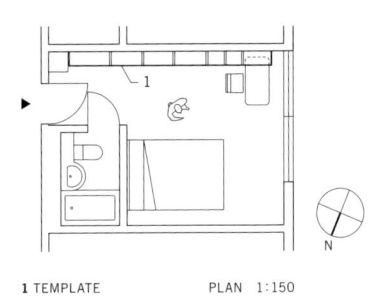

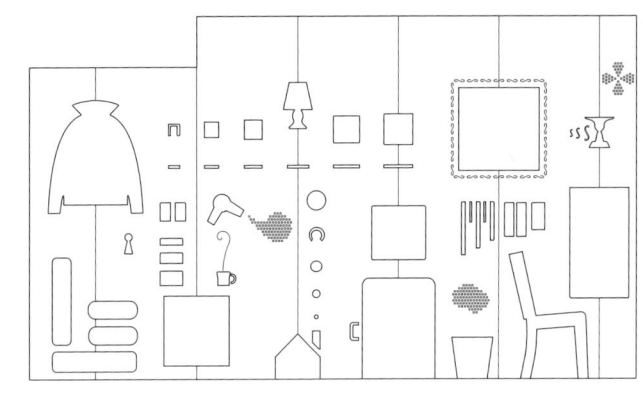

1 TEMPLATE　　　　PLAN 1:150
1 テンプレート

ELEVATION 1:50

Principle use: MONTHLY HOTEL
Design:
Koichi Suzuno + Shinya Kamuro
Lighting design: MAXRAY
Construction: IKEYA
Building site: Hotel CLASKA
Total floor area: 18m² × 3 rooms
Design period: 2004.02–03
Construction period: 2004.04

主要用途：長期滞在者用客室
設計担当：鈴野浩一＋禿 真哉
照明計画：マックスレイ
施工：IKEYA
所在：ホテル クラスカ
延床面積：18㎡×3室
設計期間：2004.02–03
施工期間：2004.04

P.18 HOUSE IN OOKAYAMA
大岡山の住宅

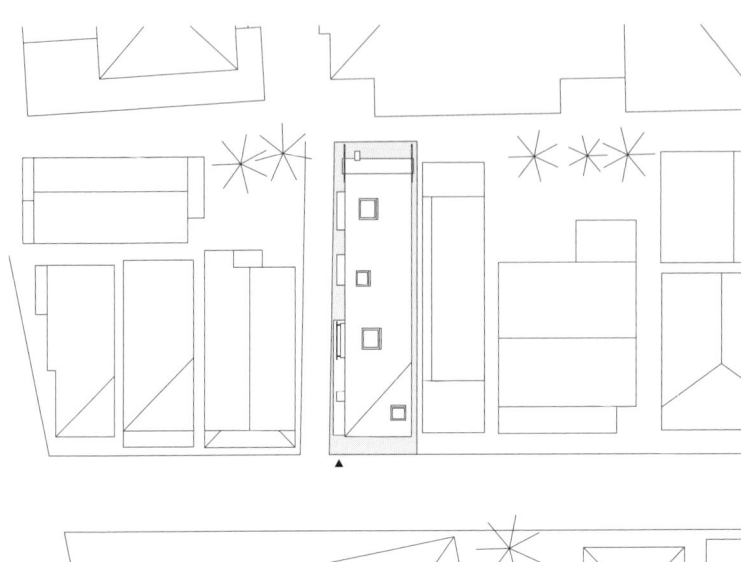

SITE PLAN 1:400

194

PROJECT DATA + DRAWINGS

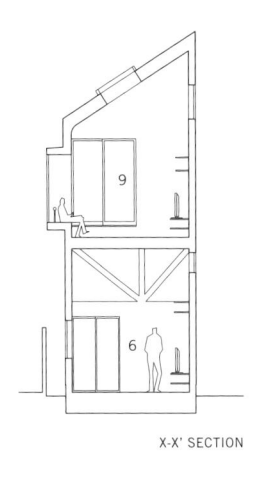

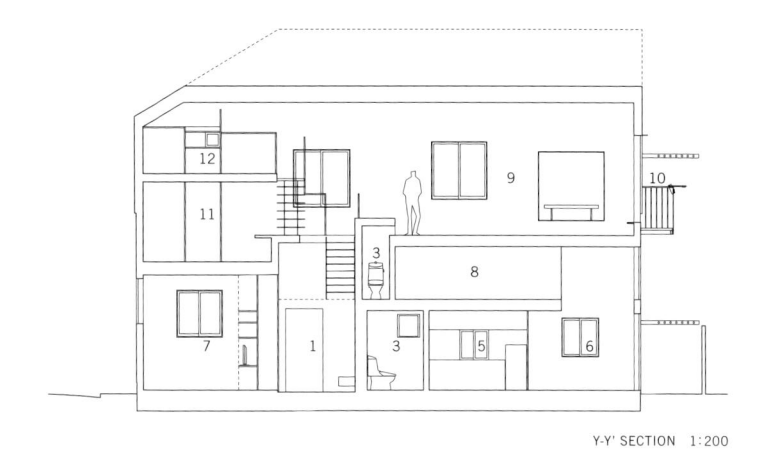

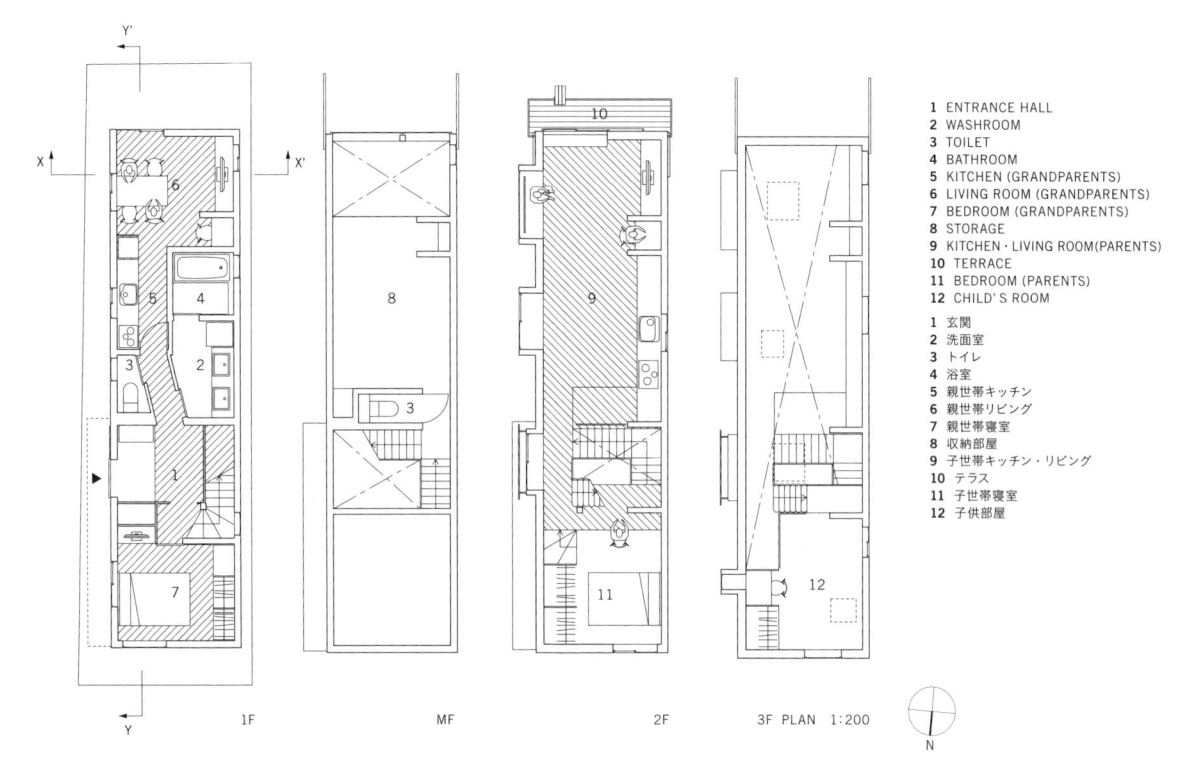

X-X' SECTION

Y-Y' SECTION 1:200

1F MF 2F 3F PLAN 1:200

1 ENTRANCE HALL
2 WASHROOM
3 TOILET
4 BATHROOM
5 KITCHEN (GRANDPARENTS)
6 LIVING ROOM (GRANDPARENTS)
7 BEDROOM (GRANDPARENTS)
8 STORAGE
9 KITCHEN · LIVING ROOM (PARENTS)
10 TERRACE
11 BEDROOM (PARENTS)
12 CHILD'S ROOM

1 玄関
2 洗面室
3 トイレ
4 浴室
5 親世帯キッチン
6 親世帯リビング
7 親世帯寝室
8 収納部屋
9 子世帯キッチン・リビング
10 テラス
11 子世帯寝室
12 子供部屋

Principle use: HOUSE
Design: Koichi Suzuno + Shinya Kamuro + Tomohiko Tashiro
Structural design: OHNO-JAPAN
Lighting design: MAXRAY
Construction: AO
Fabric design: NUNO
Building site: Meguro Tokyo
Site area: 76.2m²
Total floor area: 104.5m²
Number of stories: 3F + Storage
Structure: Wood
Design period: 2009.11–2010.05
Construction period: 2010.06–11

主要用途：住宅
設計担当：鈴野浩一＋禿 真哉＋田代朋彦
構造設計：オーノJAPAN
照明計画：マックスレイ
施工：青
ファブリック：NUNO
所在：東京 目黒
敷地面積：76.2㎡
延床面積：104.5㎡
規模：地上3階＋収納階
構造：木造
設計期間：2009.11–2010.05
施工期間：2010.06–11

TORAFU ARCHITECTS IDEA + PROCESS 2004-2011

P.24 NIKE PRESSROOM
NIKE PRESSROOM

Principle use: PRESS ROOM
Design: Koichi Suzuno +
Shinya Kamuro + Yuho Miyai
Lighting design: On&Off
Construction: ISHIMARU
Building site: Nakameguro Tokyo
Total floor area: 284.8m²
Design period: 2007.02-06
Construction period: 2007.06-07

主要用途:プレスルーム
設計担当:鈴野浩一+禿 真哉+宮井裕穂
照明計画:On&Off
施工:イシマル
所在:東京 中目黒
延床面積:284.8㎡
設計期間:2007.02-06
施工期間:2007.06-07

1 LOBBY	1 ロビー
2 MEETING ROOM	2 会議室
3 TERRACE	3 テラス
4 BRANDING AREA	4 ブランディングエリア
5 PRODUCT ROOM	5 プロダクトルーム
6 ROOM FOR STYLISTS	6 スタイリストルーム
7 OFFICE	7 オフィス
8 STORAGE	8 倉庫

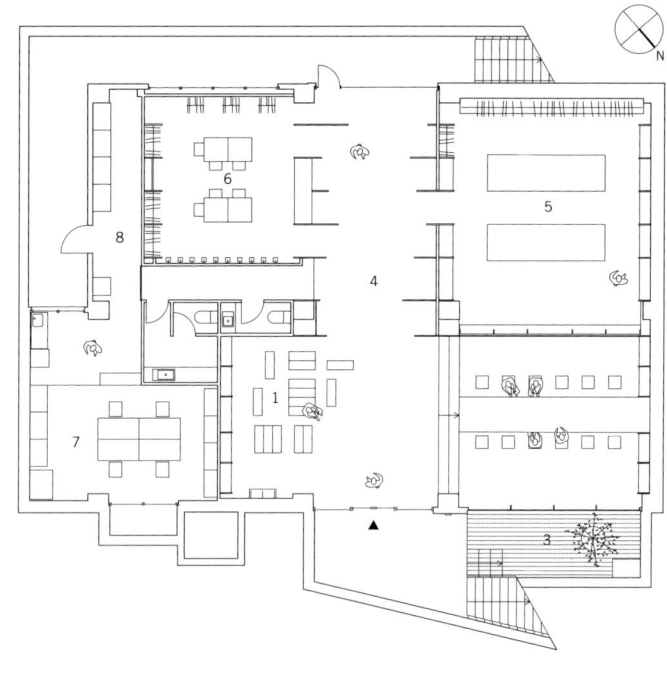

PLAN 1:250

P.28 Yuichi Yokoyama Solo Exhibition at KAWASAKI CITY MUSEUM
川崎市市民ミュージアム「横山裕一」展

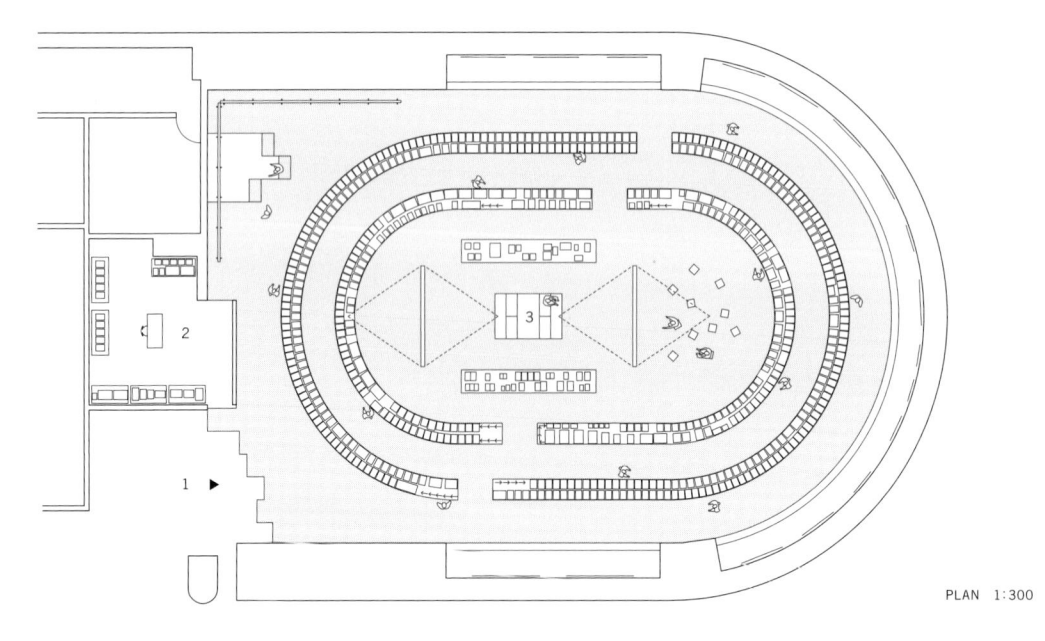

PLAN 1:300

Principle use: EXHIBITION SITE
Design: Koichi Suzuno +
Shinya Kamuro + Hanae Yamaguchi
Construction: Tokyo Studio
Building site:
KAWASAKI CITY MUSEUM
Total floor area: 582.1m²
Design period: 2010.01-04
Construction period: 2010.04
Duration: 2010.04.24-06.20

主要用途:展示会場構成
設計担当:鈴野浩一+禿 真哉+山口英恵
施工:東京スタデオ
会場:川崎市市民ミュージアム
延床面積:582.1㎡
設計期間:2010.01-04
施工期間:2010.04
会期:2010.04.24-06.20

1 ENTRANCE・EXIT
2 ARTIST'S ROOM
3 EXHIBITION ROOM

1 出入口
2 作家の部屋
3 展示室

PROJECT DATA + DRAWINGS

P.32 Pappa TARAHUMARA "PunK · Don Quixote"
パパ・タラフマラ「パンク・ドンキホーテ」

Principle use: STAGE SET
Design: Koichi Suzuno +
Shinya Kamuro + Hanae Yamaguchi
Construction: C-COM / TAKIZAWA
Building site:
OWL SPOT
Toshima Performing Arts Center
Total floor area: 116m²
Design period: 2009.07–11
Construction period: 2009.11
Duration: 2009.12.11–20

主要用途：舞台美術
設計担当：鈴野浩一＋禿 真哉＋山口英恵
施工：C-COM／滝沢金属工業
会場：豊島区立舞台芸術交流センター
あうるすぽっと
延床面積：116㎡
設計期間：2009.07–11
施工期間：2009.11
会期：2009.12.11–20

P.36 minä perhonen arkistot
ミナ ペルホネン アルキストット

Principle use: SHOP
Design: Koichi Suzuno +
Shinya Kamuro + Hanae Yamaguchi
Construction:
Tokyo Studio / MASAMUNE
Building site: Shirokanedai Tokyo
Total floor area: 97.2m²
Design period: 2010.06–09
Construction period: 2010.08–09

主要用途：物販店舗
設計担当：鈴野浩一＋禿 真哉＋山口英恵
施工：東京スタデオ／正棟建築
所在：東京 白金台
延床面積：97.2㎡
設計期間：2010.06–09
施工期間：2010.08–09

1 CASHIER
2 SHOP
3 FITTING ROOM
4 STORAGE
5 OFFICE

1 レジカウンター
2 売場
3 フィッティングルーム
4 倉庫
5 オフィス

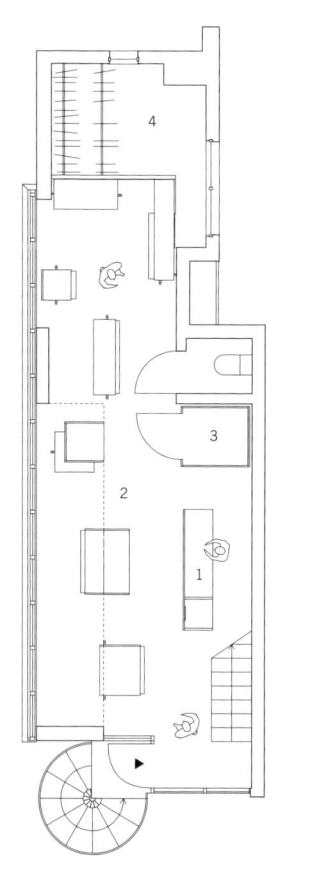

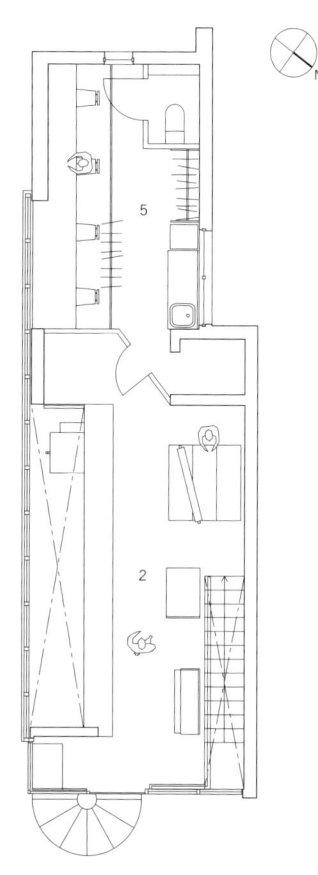

2F　　3F PLAN 1:150

P.40 Kitchen Blocks
キッチンの積み木

Principle use: PRODUCT
Design:
Koichi Suzuno + Hisamichi Iizuka
Production: IZUTSU-YA
Material: Hinoki
Size: W217×D217×H50mm
Design period: 2010.05–10
Production period: 2010.05–10

主要用途：プロダクト
設計担当：鈴野浩一＋飯塚之通
製作：井筒屋
素材：ヒノキ
サイズ：W217×D217×H50㎜
設計期間：2010.05–10
製作期間：2010.05–10

TORAFU ARCHITECTS IDEA + PROCESS 2004-2011

P.44 HOUSE IN KOHOKU
港北の住宅

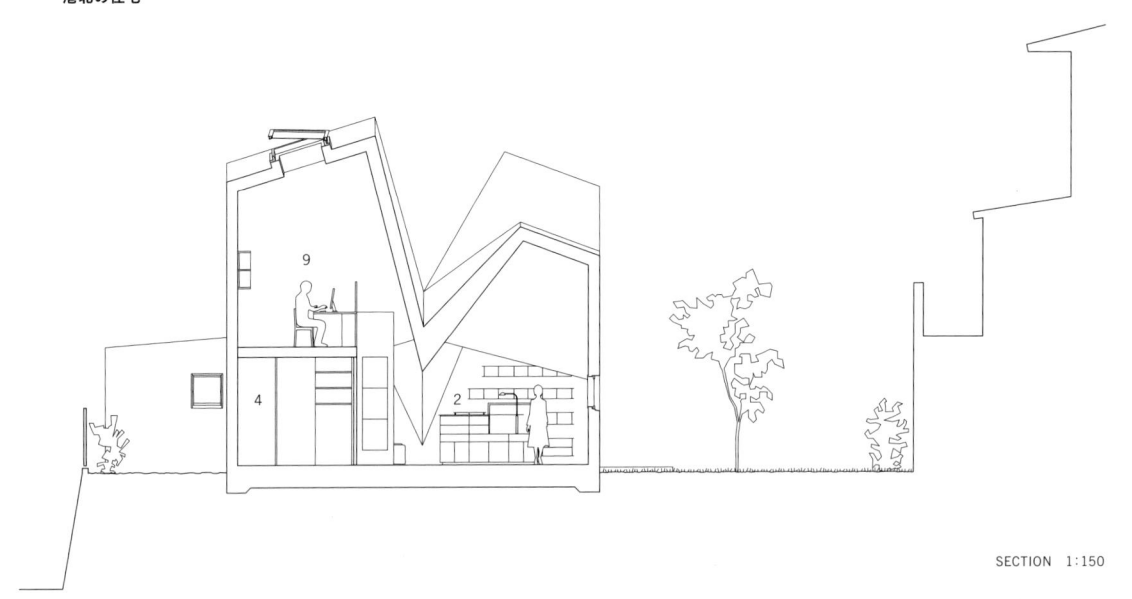

SECTION 1:150

Principle use: HOUSE
Design:
Koichi Suzuno + Shinya Kamuro
Structural design:
MID architectural structure laboratory
Lighting design: spangle
Construction: YAMASHO
Furniture design collaboration:
TAIJI FUJIMORI ATELIER
Fabric design: NUNO
Building site: Yokohama Kanagawa
Site area: 230.8m²
Total floor area: 67.4m²
Number of stories: 1F + Loft
Structure: RC
Design period: 2007.01-11
Construction period:
2007.12-2008.07

主要用途：住宅
設計担当：鈴野浩一＋禿 真哉
構造設計：MID研究所
照明計画：スパンコール
施工：山庄建設
家具共同設計：藤森泰司アトリエ
ファブリック：NUNO
所在：神奈川 横浜
敷地面積：230.8㎡
延床面積：67.4㎡
規模：地上1階＋ロフト
構造：鉄筋コンクリート造
設計期間：2007.01-11
施工期間：2007.12-2008.07

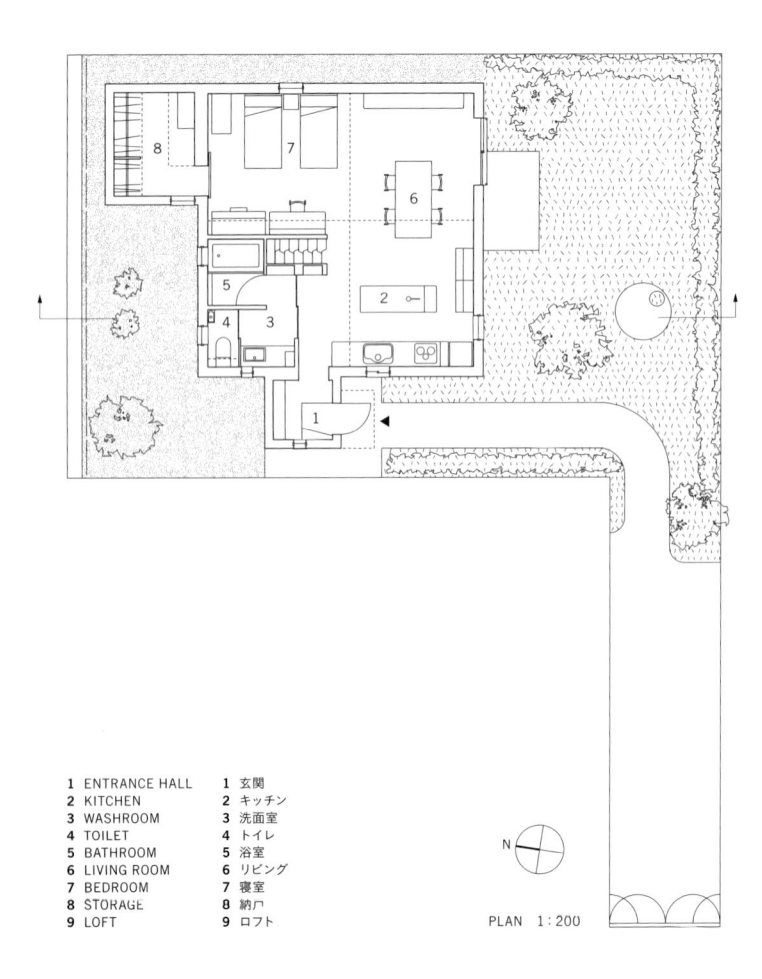

1 ENTRANCE HALL	1 玄関
2 KITCHEN	2 キッチン
3 WASHROOM	3 洗面室
4 TOILET	4 トイレ
5 BATHROOM	5 浴室
6 LIVING ROOM	6 リビング
7 BEDROOM	7 寝室
8 STORAGE	8 納戸
9 LOFT	9 ロフト

PLAN 1:200

PROJECT DATA + DRAWINGS

P.52 Y150 NISSAN PAVILION
Y150 NISSAN パビリオン

Principle use: EXHIBITION SITE
Design: Koichi Suzuno +
Shinya Kamuro + Naohiro Nakamura
Construction: MURAYAMA
Producer: TBWA\HAKUHODO
Planning & Direction: HAKUHODO
Signage design:
Hideyuki Yamano Graphic Design
Building site: Shinko Pier Yokohama
Total floor area: 2196m²
Design period: 2008.09–2009.02
Construction period: 2009.03–04
Duration: 2009.04.28–09.27

主要用途：展示会場構成
設計担当：鈴野浩一＋禿 真哉＋中村尚弘
施工：ムラヤマ
プロデュース：TBWA\HAKUHODO
企画・総合演出：博報堂
サイン計画：
山野英之グラフィックデザイン
会場：横浜 新港埠頭
延床面積：2196㎡
設計期間：2008.09–2009.02
施工期間：2009.03–04
会期：2009.04.28–09.27

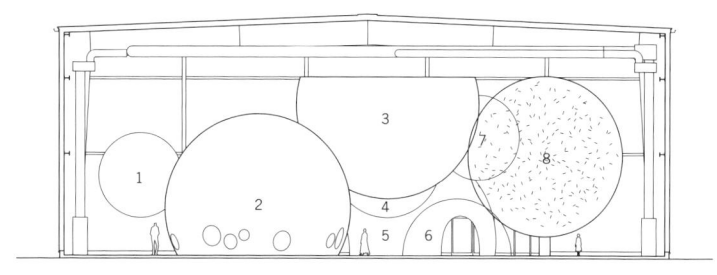

SECTION 1:400

1 Lighting sphere φ4500
2 White – Piezoelectric light φ10000
3 White – Pendant φ10000
4 Transparent φ6000
5 Exit sphere φ11500
6 Transparent φ6000 hemisphere (floor: mirrors)
7 Lighting sphere φ4500
8 " Dancing Leaves" sphere φ8500

1 照明球 φ4500
2 白・床発電 φ10000
3 白・吊下げ φ10000
4 透明 φ6000
5 出口球 φ11500
6 透明 φ6000半球（床：ミラー）
7 照明球 φ4500
8 舞球 φ8500

P.58 Light Loom (Canon Milano Salone 2011)
光の織機 (Canon Milano Salone 2011)

Principle use: EXHIBITION SITE
Design: Koichi Suzuno +
Shinya Kamuro + Kazunori Arihara
Visual design: WOW
Construction: Taiyo Kogyo
Producer: TRUNK
Supervisor: ZITOMORI
Building site: Superstudio Più
ART POINT, Tortona, Milano Italy
Total floor area: 825m²
Design period: 2010.09–2011.03
Construction period: 2011.04.01–10
Duration: 2011.04.12–17

主要用途：展示会場構成
設計担当：鈴野浩一＋禿 真哉＋有原寿典
ヴィジュアルデザイン：WOW
施工：太陽工業
プロデュース：TRUNK
監修：ZITOMORI
会場：イタリア ミラノ トルトーナ地区
スーパースタジオ・ピュー内 ART POINT
延床面積：825㎡
設計期間：2010.09–2011.03
施工期間：2011.04.01–10
会期：2011.04.12–17

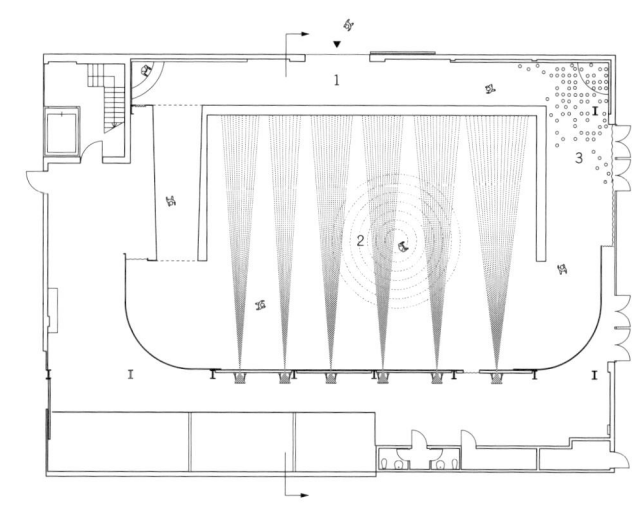

PLAN 1:450

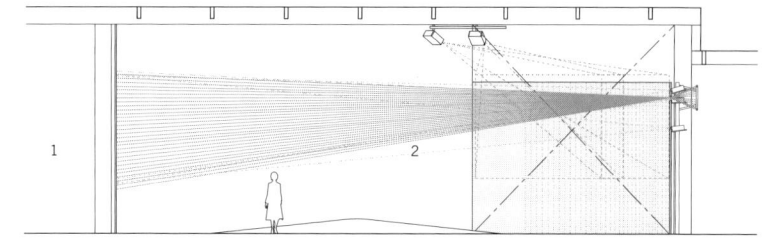

1 ENTRANCE・EXIT
2 EXHIBITION ROOM
3 SHOWROOM

1 出入口
2 展示室
3 ショールーム

SECTION 1:200

TORAFU ARCHITECTS IDEA + PROCESS 2004-2011

P.64　HermanMiller Store Tokyo
ハーマンミラーストア東京

Principle use: SHOP
Design: Koichi Suzuno +
Shinya Kamuro + Eikichi Saku
Lighting design: USHIOSPAX
Construction: ISHIMARU
Signage design: TAKAIYAMA inc.
Building site: Marunouchi Tokyo
Total floor area: 197.9m²
Design period: 2010.07-10
Construction period: 2010.10-11

主要用途：物販店舗
設計担当：鈴野浩一＋禿 真哉＋朔 永吉
照明計画：ウシオスペックス
施工：イシマル
サイン計画：高い山
所在：東京 丸の内
延床面積：197.9㎡
設計期間：2010.07-10
施工期間：2010.10-11

1　SHOP
2　CASHIER

1　売場
2　レジカウンター

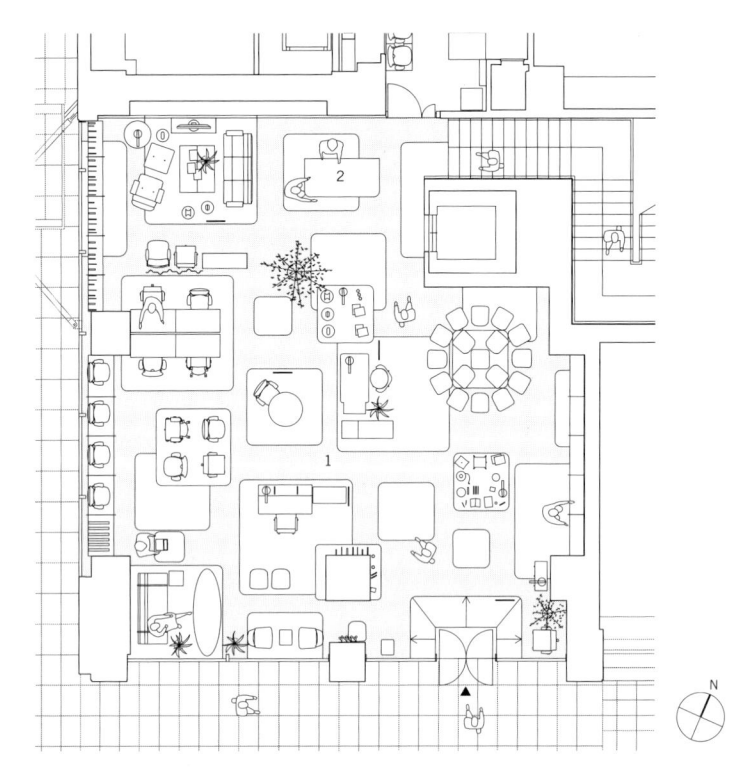

PLAN 1:200

P.68　SPINNING OBJECTS
回転体

Principle use: SHOWROOM
Design:
Koichi Suzuno + Shinya Kamuro
Lighting design: MAXRAY
Construction: DAIKIART FACTORY /
INOUE INDUSTRIES (SPINNING
OBJECTS)
Furniture design collaboration:
TAIJI FUJIMORI ATELIER
Building site: Fuchu Tokyo
Total floor area: 167m²
Design period: 2004.05-09
Construction period: 2004.09-10

主要用途：ショールーム
設計担当：鈴野浩一＋禿 真哉
照明計画：マックスレイ
施工：ダイキ・アート製作所／
イノウエインダストリィズ（回転体）
家具共同設計：藤森泰司アトリエ
所在：東京 府中
延床面積：167㎡
設計期間：2004.05-09
施工期間：2004.09-10

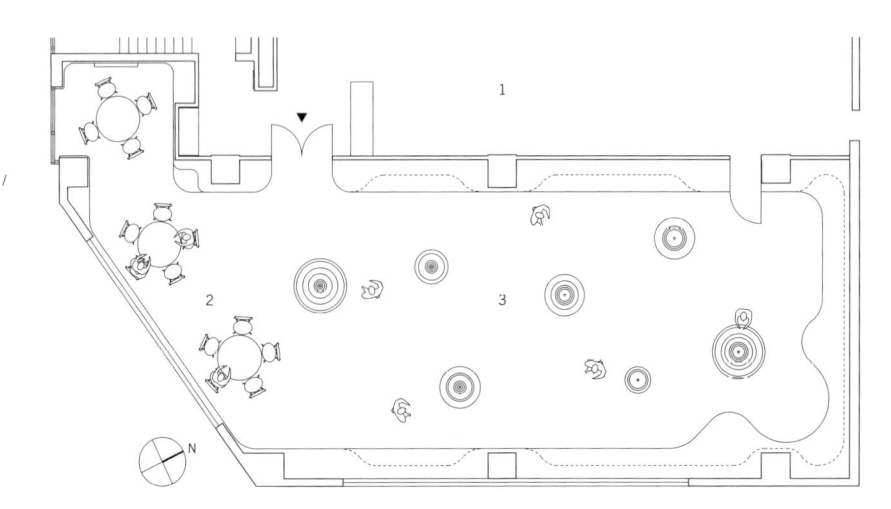

1　OFFICE　　　　1　オフィス
2　MEETING SPACE　2　ミーティングスペース
3　SHOWROOM　　3　ショールーム

PLAN 1:200

PROJECT DATA + DRAWINGS

P.72 EXHIBITION UNDERGROUND
地下展 UNDERGROUND

1 ENTRANCE
2 EXHIBITION ROOM
3 EXIT

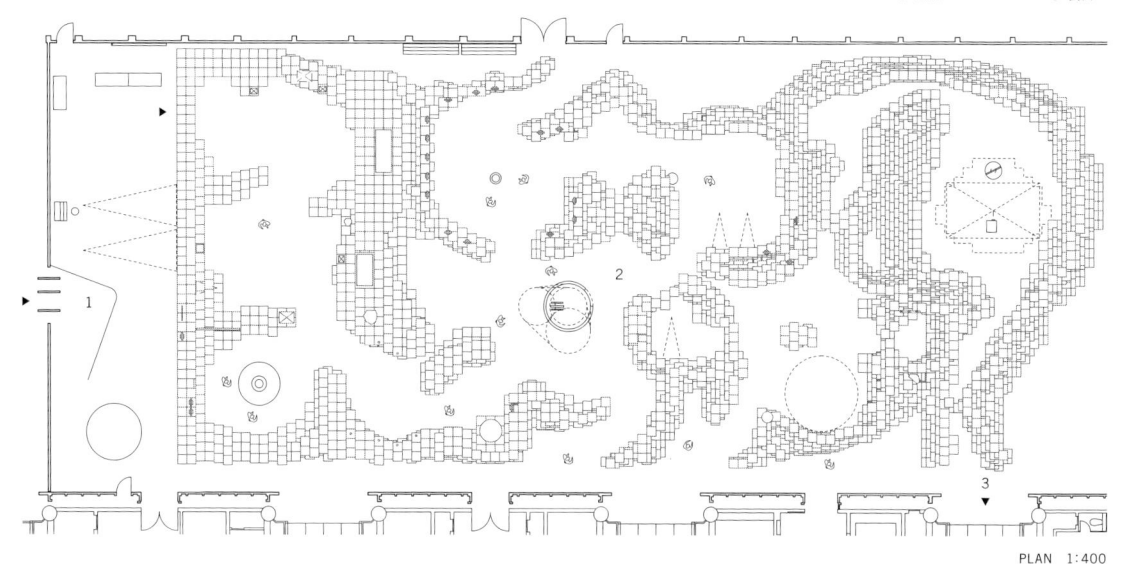

1 入口
2 展示室
3 出口

PLAN 1:400

Principle use: EXHIBITION SITE
Design: Koichi Suzuno +
Shinya Kamuro + Ritsuko Ameno
Lighting design:
Izumi Okayasu Lighting Design
Construction:
INOUE INDUSTRIES / ISHIMARU
Exhibition design:
BOCTOK / SOUP DESIGN

Fabric design: NUNO
Building site:
The National Museum of Emerging
Science and Innovation, Japan
Total floor area: 1600m²
Design period: 2006.11–2007.04
Construction period: 2007.09.06–20
Duration: 2007.09.22–2008.01.28

主要用途：展示会場構成
設計担当：
鈴野浩一＋禿 真哉＋飴野りつ子
照明計画：岡安泉照明設計事務所
施工：
イノウエインダストリィズ／イシマル
展示：ボストーク／スープ・デザイン
ファブリック：NUNO

会場：日本科学未来館
延床面積：1600㎡
設計期間：2006.11–2007.04
施工期間：2007.09.06–20
会期：2007.09.22–2008.01.28

P.76 HOUSE IN NAKAMARU
中丸の住宅

Principle use: HOUSE
Design: Koichi Suzuno +
Shinya Kamuro + Tomohiko Tashiro
Structural design: Yasushi Moribe,
Showa Women's University
Lighting design: spangle
Construction: CHUBACHI
Fabric design: NUNO
Building site: Yokohama Kanagawa
Site area: 74.5m²
Total floor area: 78.9m²
Number of stories: 2F
Structure: Wood
Design period: 2008.05–10
Construction period:
2008.11–2009.05

主要用途：住宅
設計担当：鈴野浩一＋禿 真哉＋田代朋彦
構造設計：昭和女子大学 森部康司
照明計画：スパンコール
施工：中鉢建設
ファブリック：NUNO
所在：神奈川 横浜
敷地面積：74.5㎡
延床面積：78.9㎡
規模：地上2階
構造：木造
設計期間：2008.05–10
施工期間：2008.11–2009.05

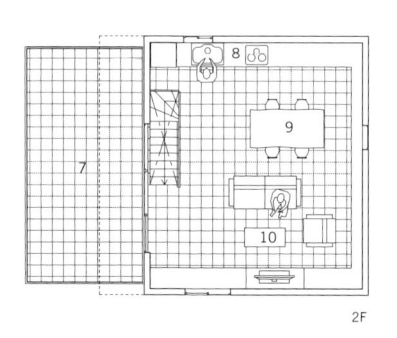

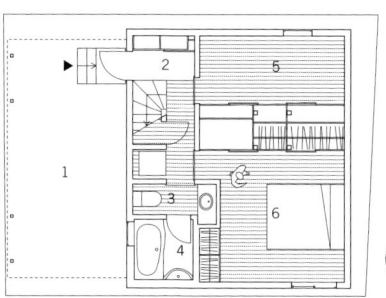

ELEVATION 1:300

2F

1F PLAN 1:200

1 PARKING SPACE	1 駐車スペース
2 ENTRANCE HALL	2 玄関
3 WASHROOM・TOILET	3 洗面室・トイレ
4 BATHROOM	4 浴室
5 STORAGE	5 納戸
6 BEDROOM	6 寝室
7 TERRACE	7 テラス
8 KITCHEN	8 キッチン
9 DINING ROOM	9 ダイニング
10 LIVING ROOM	10 リビング

TORAFU ARCHITECTS IDEA + PROCESS 2004-2011

P.78 TORANOANA AKIHABARA
とらのあな AKIHABARA

Principle use: SHOP
Design:
Koichi Suzuno + Shinya Kamuro
Construction: TANSEI TDC
Building site: Akihabara Tokyo
Total floor area: 84.6m²
Design period: 2006.04-06
Construction period: 2006.06-07

主要用途:物販店舗
設計担当:鈴野浩一＋禿 真哉
施工:丹青TDC
所在:東京 秋葉原
延床面積:84.6㎡
設計期間:2006.04-06
施工期間:2006.06-07

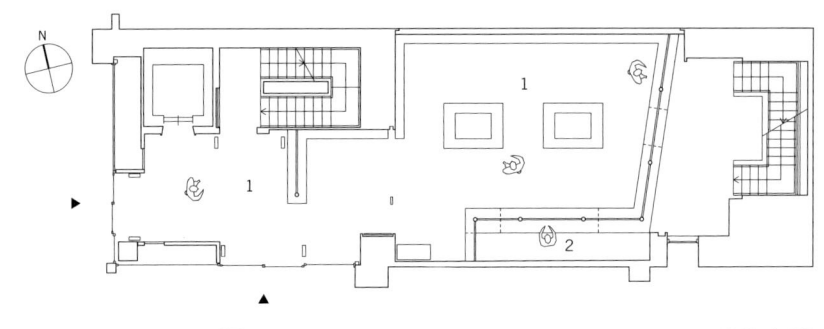

1 SHOP　　1 売場
2 CASHIER　2 レジカウンター
PLAN 1:200

P.79 EGG ZABUTON
エッグ座布団

Principle use: EXHIBITED WORK
Design: Koichi Suzuno +
Shinya Kamuro + Yuho Miyai
Production: A·PLANNING
Material: High density low-repulsion polyurethane foam
Size: W300×D300×H55mm
Building site: BankART1929 Yokohama
Design period: 2006.01-02
Production period: 2006.02
Duration: 2006.02.24-03.14

主要用途:展覧会作品
設計担当:鈴野浩一＋禿 真哉＋宮井裕穂
製作:A·PLANNING
素材:高密度低反発ウレタンフォーム
サイズ:W300×D300×H55mm
会場:BankART1929 Yokohama
設計期間:2006.01-02
製作期間:2006.02
会期:2006.02.24-03.14

P.88 NEW PEOPLE
NEW PEOPLE

Principle use:
SHOP / OFFICE / GALLERY
Design:
Koichi Suzuno + Shinya Kamuro
Lighting design:
Izumi Okayasu Lighting Design
Construction: ISHIMARU
Design collaboration:
TAIJI FUJIMORI ATELIER
Signage design: TAKAIYAMA inc.
Art work: Yuichi Yokoyama / Noritake
Fabric design: NUNO
Building site: San Francisco USA
Total floor area: 194.8m²
Design period: 2008.04-12
Construction period: 2009.01-08

主要用途:
物販店舗／オフィス／ギャラリー
設計担当:鈴野浩一＋禿 真哉
照明計画:岡安泉照明設計事務所
施工:イシマル
共同設計:藤森泰司アトリエ
サイン計画:高い山
アートワーク:横山裕一／のりたけ
ファブリック:NUNO
所在:アメリカ サンフランシスコ
延床面積:194.8㎡
設計期間:2008.04-12
施工期間:2009.01-08

1 SHOP　　1 売場
2 CASHIER　2 レジカウンター
PLAN 1:200

PROJECT DATA + DRAWINGS

ELEVATION   SECTION 1:30

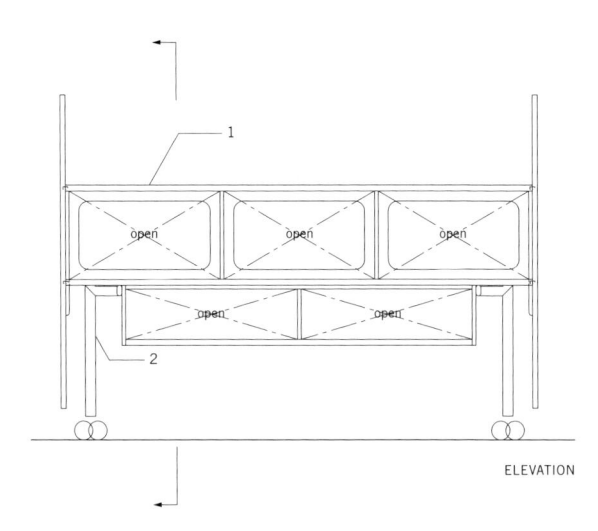

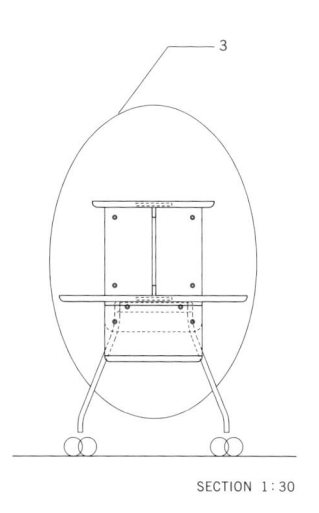

1. Shelves: MDF (softwood type)
   t=24mm, 15mm
   White dye under clear urethane coating
2. Leg frame:
   ST ellipsoidal pipe 48mm × 20mm × (t=1.6mm)
   Melamine resin baked into coating
3. Face panel: MDF (softwood type) t ≒ 21mm
   " Face" artwork on adhesive sheet applied to top surface

1. 本体棚部：MDF材（針葉樹タイプ）
   t＝24mm、15mm
   白染色の上クリアウレタン塗装
2. 脚フレーム：
   ST長円パイプ 48mm×20mm×（t＝1.6mm）
   メラミン樹脂焼付塗装
3. 顔パネル：MDF材（針葉樹タイプ）t ≒ 21mm
   トップ面に「顔」シート貼り

P.94 Exhibition of minä perhonen
ミナ ペルホネンのエキシビション

Principle use: DISPLAY BOOTH
Construction: Tokyo Studio
Building site:
ISETAN SHINJUKU 1F "The Stage"
Total floor area: 77.8m²

主要用途：展示ブース
施工：東京スタデオ
会場：
伊勢丹新宿店本館1階ザ・ステージ
延床面積：77.8㎡

1. minä perhonen "Rainwear In / Rainwear Out"
ミナ ペルホネン「雨のウチ・ソト」

Design: Koichi Suzuno +
Shinya Kamuro + Hanae Yamaguchi
Design period: 2009.04–06
Construction period: 2009.06.02
Duration: 2009.06.03–09

設計担当：鈴野浩一＋禿 真哉＋山口英恵
設計期間：2009.04–06
施工期間：2009.06.02
会期：2009.06.03–09

2. minä perhonen and Life Design
ミナ ペルホネンと生活デザイン

Design: Koichi Suzuno +
Shinya Kamuro + Yuho Miyai
Design period: 2008.05–07
Construction period: 2008.07.08
Duration: 2008.07.09–15

設計担当：鈴野浩一＋禿 真哉＋宮井裕穂
設計期間：2008.05–07
施工期間：2008.07.08
会期：2008.07.09–15

3. Lifestyle of minä perhonen
ライフスタイル オブ ミナ ペルホネン

Design: Koichi Suzuno +
Shinya Kamuro + Yuho Miyai
Design period: 2007.04–06
Construction period: 2007.06.05
Duration: 2007.06.06–12

設計担当：鈴野浩一＋禿 真哉＋宮井裕穂
設計期間：2007.04–06
施工期間：2007.06.05
会期：2007.06.06–12

P.96 3M store
3M ストア

Principle use: SHOP / SHOWROOM
Design: Koichi Suzuno +
Shinya Kamuro + Hanae Yamaguchi
Lighting design:
Izumi Okayasu Lighting Design
Construction: ISHIMARU / WAKO /
Asai Marking System
Planning, Producer and Contents creation: B2engine
Art work: Kiyoshi Kuroda
Building site: Omotesando Tokyo
Total floor area: 236.8m²
Design period: 2010.04–08
Construction period: 2010.06–08
Duration: 2010.08–12

主要用途：物販店舗／ショールーム
設計担当：鈴野浩一＋禿 真哉＋山口英恵
照明計画：岡安泉照明設計事務所
施工：イシマル／和光／
アサイマーキングシステム
企画・プロデュース・コンテンツ企画制作：
B2エンジン
アートワーク：黒田 潔
所在：東京 表参道
延床面積：236.8㎡
設計期間：2010.04–08
施工期間：2010.06–08
会期：2010.08–12

TORAFU ARCHITECTS IDEA + PROCESS 2004-2011

P.98 yozakura (Kaneka Milano Salone 2011)
yozakura (Kaneka Milano Salone 2011)

Principle use: EXHIBITION SITE
Design: Koichi Suzuno +
Shinya Kamuro + Jody Wong
Lighting design:
Izumi Okayasu Lighting Design
Construction: NOMURA
Producer: NOMURA
Art work: wabisabi for Dezain
Building site: Superstudio Più
MYOWNGALLERY, Tortona, Milano Italy
Total floor area: 287m²
Design period: 2010.10–2011.03
Construction period: 2011.01–04
Duration: 2011.04.12–17

主要用途：展示会場構成
設計担当：鈴野浩一＋禿 真哉＋
ジョディ・ウォン
照明計画：岡安泉照明設計事務所
施工：乃村工藝社
プロデュース：乃村工藝社
アートワーク：デザ院（ワビサビ）
会場：イタリア ミラノ トルトーナ地区
スーパースタジオ・ピュー内
MYOWNGALLERY
延床面積：287㎡
設計期間：2010.10–2011.03
施工期間：2011.01–04
会期：2011.04.12–17

P.102 GREGORY TOKYO STORE
GREGORY TOKYO STORE

Principle use: SHOP
Design: Koichi Suzuno +
Shinya Kamuro + Tomohiko Tashiro
Lighting design: On&Off
Construction: ISHIMARU / Mihoya Glass
Signage design:
Hideyuki Yamano Graphic Design
Building site: Harajuku Tokyo
Total floor area: 64.4m²
Design period: 2008.03–06
Construction period: 2008.06

主要用途：物販店舗
設計担当：鈴野浩一＋禿 真哉＋田代朋彦
照明計画：On&Off
施工：イシマル／三保谷硝子店
サイン計画：
山野英之グラフィックデザイン
所在：東京 原宿
延床面積：64.4㎡
設計期間：2008.03–06
施工期間：2008.06

1 BENCH	1 丸太ベンチ
2 SIGNAGE	2 標識
3 STAIRS	3 既存階段
4 TREES	4 既存樹木
5 SHOP	5 売場
6 CASHIER	6 レジカウンター

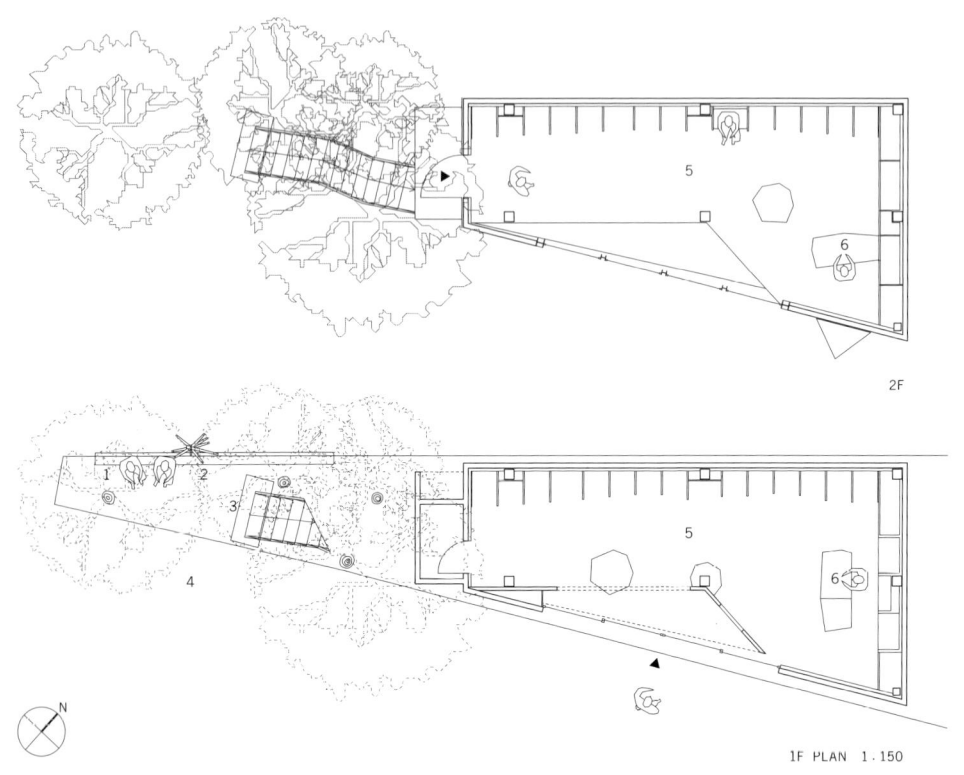

2F

1F PLAN 1:150

PROJECT DATA + DRAWINGS

P.104 NIKE 1LOVE
NIKE 1LOVE

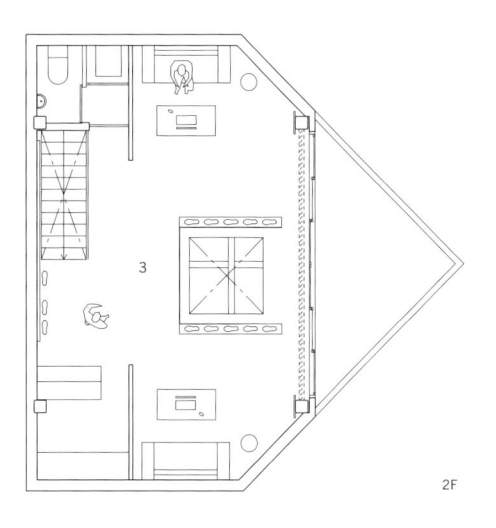

2F

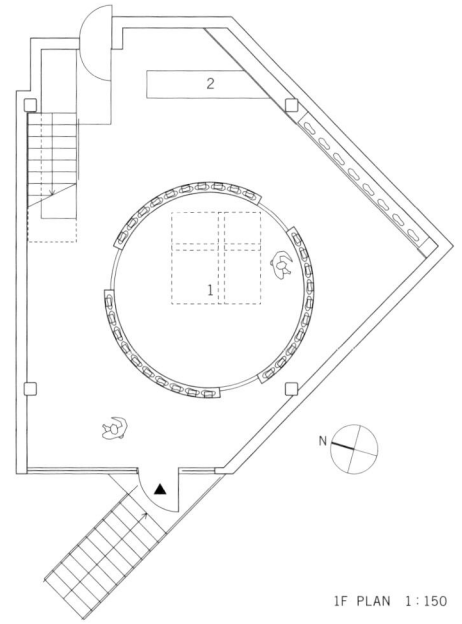

1F PLAN 1:150

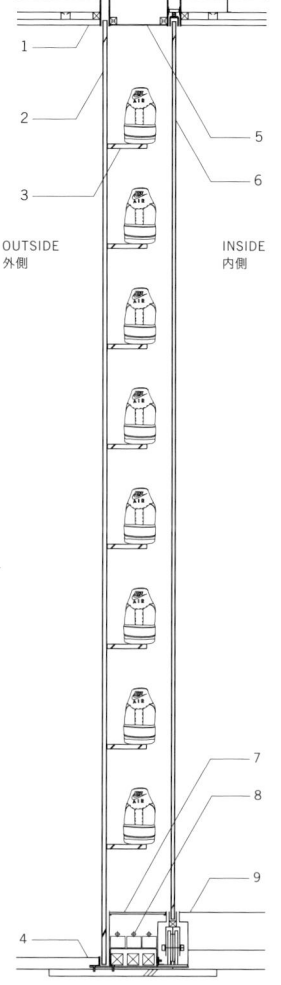

OUTSIDE 外側   INSIDE 内側

1 Cemented excelsior board: t=15mm AEP White coating, matte finish
2 Transparent glass: t=12mm
3 High transmittance glass bracket: t=12mm
4 Mortar floor with trowel finish t=35mm
5 Stainless steel mirror finish: t=1.5mm
6 Sliding transparent glass door: t=10mm
7 Milky acrylic: t=5mm
8 Bent FL fluorescent tube
9 Mortar floor with trowel finish raised with styrene foam mortar: t=100mm

1 木毛セメント板：t＝15㎜ AEP白塗装ツヤ無
2 透明ガラス：t＝12㎜
3 高透過ガラスブラケット：t＝12㎜
4 床モルタル金ゴテ仕上：t＝35㎜
5 ステンレス鏡面仕上げ：t＝1.5㎜
6 引き戸透明ガラス：t＝10㎜
7 乳半アクリル：t＝5㎜
8 曲げFL蛍光管
9 スタイロフォーム下地 モルタル金ゴテ仕上：t＝100㎜

1 SHOP
2 CASHIER
3 NIKE iD STUDIO

1 売場
2 レジカウンター
3 NIKE iD STUDIO

SECTION OF GLASS SHOWCASE
ガラスショーケース断面図
1:20

Principle use: SHOP
Design: Koichi Suzuno + Shinya Kamuro + Yuho Miyai
Lighting design: On&Off
Construction: ISHIMARU / Mihoya Glass
Building site: Harajuku Tokyo
Total floor area: 108m²
Design period: 2006.11–12
Construction period: 2006.12–2007.01
Duration: 2007.01–2008.01

主要用途：物販店舗
設計担当：鈴野浩一＋禿 真哉＋宮井裕穂
照明計画：On&Off
施工：イシマル／三保谷硝子店
所在：東京 原宿
延床面積：108㎡
設計期間：2006.11–12
施工期間：2006.12–2007.01
会期：2007.01–2008.01

P.110 CARBON HOLDER
炭素ホルダー

Principle use: PRODUCT
Design: Koichi Suzuno + Shinya Kamuro
Mechanical design: Tetsuya Fujitani
Production: Tetsuya Fujitani / OG FACTORY
Material: Carbon
Size: φ12×H130mm
Design period: 2008.10–12
Production period: 2009.01–02

主要用途：プロダクト
設計担当：鈴野浩一＋禿 真哉
機構部設計：藤谷哲也
製作：藤谷哲也／オージーファクトリー
素材：カーボン
サイズ：φ12×H130㎜
設計期間：2008.10–12
製作期間：2009.01–02

P.110 SKY HOUSE
スカイハウス

Principle use: EXHIBITION SITE
Design: Koichi Suzuno + Shinya Kamuro + Naofumi Nanba
Construction: Kind
Building site: R-STUDIO OMOTESANDO HILLS
Design period: 2006.07–08
Construction period: 2006.08
Duration: 2006.08.24–27

主要用途：展示会場構成
設計担当：鈴野浩一＋禿 真哉＋難波真史
施工：カインド
会場：表参道ヒルズ R-STUDIO
設計期間：2006.07–08
施工期間：2006.08
会期：2006.08.24–27

TORAFU ARCHITECTS IDEA + PROCESS 2004-2011

P.112 NIKE JMC
NIKE JMC

Principle use:
OFFICE / EXHIBITION SPACE
Design: Koichi Suzuno +
Shinya Kamuro + Eikichi Saku
Lighting design: ENDO /
Hyper Active Studio (2F Auditorium)
Construction: TOA / ISHIMARU /
ITOKI MARKET SPACE
Furniture: E&Y / inter office /
UCHIDA YOKO
Project management:
PAE Design and Facility Management
Signage design: TAKAIYAMA inc.
Art work: Takeshi Abe
Building site: Tokyo Bayside
Total floor area: 5,684.8m²
Number of stories: 5F
Structure: SRC
Design period: 2008.12–2009.07
Construction period: 2009.07–09

主要用途：オフィス／展示会場
設計担当：鈴野浩一＋禿 真哉＋朔 永吉
照明計画：遠藤照明／ハイパーアクティブ
スタジオ (2F オーディトリアム)
施工：東亜建設工業／イシマル／
イトーキマーケットスペース
家具：E&Y／インターオフィス／内田洋行
プロジェクトマネージメント：
PAE Design and Facility Management
サイン計画：高い山
アートワーク：阿部岳史
所在：東京 湾岸エリア
延床面積：5,684.8㎡
規模：地上5階
構造：鉄骨鉄筋コンクリート造
設計期間：2008.12–2009.07
施工期間：2009.07–09

1 PARKING SPACE
2 RECEPTION・LOBBY
3 OFFICE
4 STAIRS
5 OFFICE
6 SERVICE AREA
7 STORAGE
8 LOADING AREA
9 LOUNGE
10 MEETING ROOM
11 PANTRY
12 AUDITORIUM
13 AV ROOM

1 駐車スペース
2 受付・ロビー
3 オフィス
4 階段室
5 事務・管理室
6 バックヤード
7 倉庫
8 荷受スペース
9 ラウンジ
10 会議室
11 パントリー
12 オーディトリアム
13 AVルーム

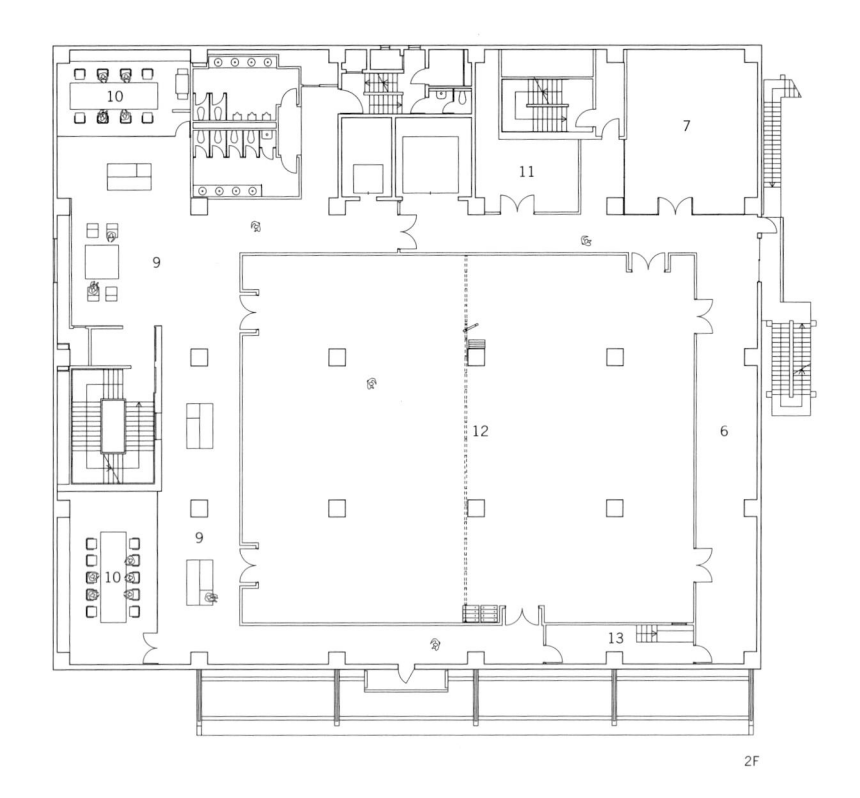

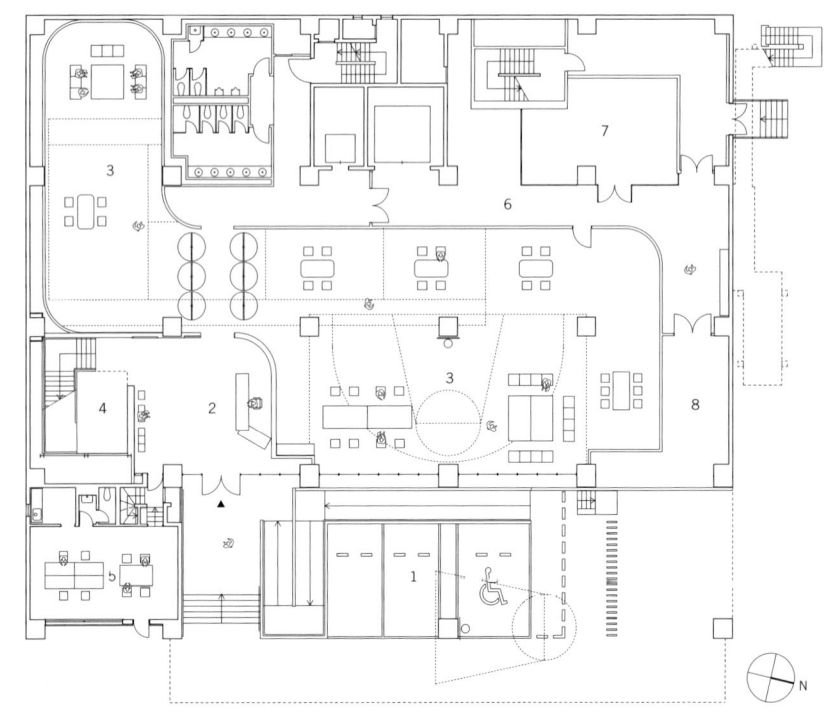

2F

1F PLAN 1 : 400

P.120 1-10design Kyoto Office
1→10design 京都オフィス

Principle use: OFFICE
Design: Koichi Suzuno +
Shinya Kamuro + Eikichi Saku
Construction: ISHIMARU
Furniture: TAIJI FUJIMORI ATELIER
Fabric design: NUNO
Building site: Karasuma Kyoto
Total floor area: 462.6m²
Design period: 2010.12–2011.02
Construction period: 2011.02–03

主要用途：オフィス
設計担当：鈴野浩一＋禿 真哉＋朔 永吉
施工：イシマル
家具：藤森泰司アトリエ
ファブリック：NUNO
所在：京都 烏丸
延床面積：462.6㎡
設計期間：2010.12–2011.02
施工期間：2011.02–03

1 RECEPTION
2 LOBBY・GALLERY
3 WORKSPACE
4 FOOTWEAR SPACE
5 MEETING ROOM
6 RESTING ROOM
7 SERVER ROOM
8 STORAGE
9 LABORATORY
10 PRESIDENT'S OFFICE
11 PRESIDENT'S RESTING ROOM

1 受付
2 ロビー・ギャラリー
3 執務スペース
4 下足スペース
5 会議室
6 休憩室
7 サーバールーム
8 倉庫
9 ラボラトリー
10 社長室／秘書室
11 社長休憩室

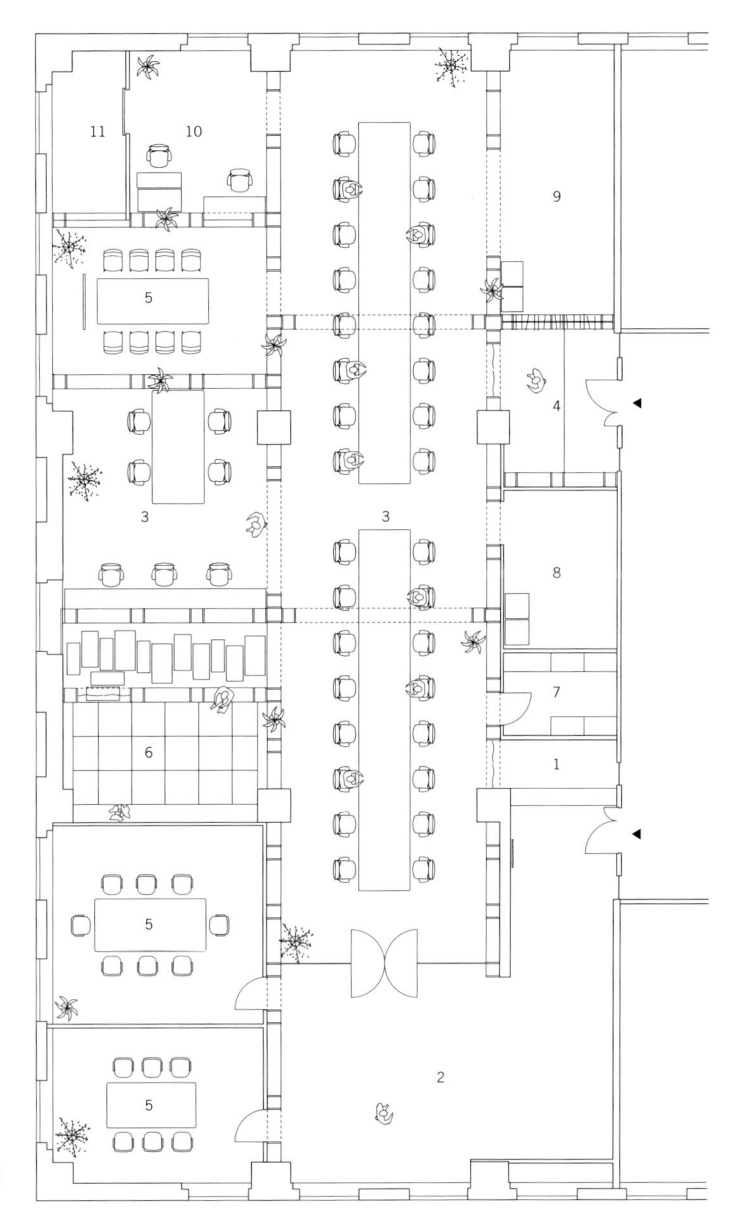

PLAN 1:200

TORAFU ARCHITECTS IDEA + PROCESS 2004-2011

P.124 KAYAC Ebisu Office
面白法人カヤック 恵比寿オフィス

Principle use: OFFICE
Design: Koichi Suzuno +
Shinya Kamuro + Hanae Yamaguchi
Construction: ISHIMARU / E&Y
Building site: Ebisu Tokyo
Total floor area: 249.9m²
Design period: 2010.11-12
Construction period: 2011.01-02

主要用途：オフィス
設計担当：鈴野浩一＋禿 真哉＋山口英恵
施工：イシマル／E&Y
所在：東京 恵比寿
延床面積：249.9㎡
設計期間：2010.11-12
施工期間：2011.01-02

1 WORKSPACE
2 MEETING ROOM
3 COPY SPACE
4 SERVER SPACE
5 STORAGE

1 執務スペース
2 会議室
3 コピースペース
4 サーバースペース
5 倉庫

PLAN 1:200

P.126 UDS Shanghai Office
UDS 上海オフィス

Principle use: OFFICE
Design:
Koichi Suzuno + Shinya Kamuro
Construction:
SHANGHAI VESSEL DESIGN &
ENGINEERING
Building site: Shanghai China
Total floor area: 86.4m²
Design period: 2005.08-10
Construction period: 2005.11

主要用途：オフィス
設計担当：鈴野浩一＋禿 真哉
施工：SHANGHAI VESSEL DESIGN &
ENGINEERING
所在：中国 上海
延床面積：86.4㎡
設計期間：2005.08-10
施工期間：2005.11

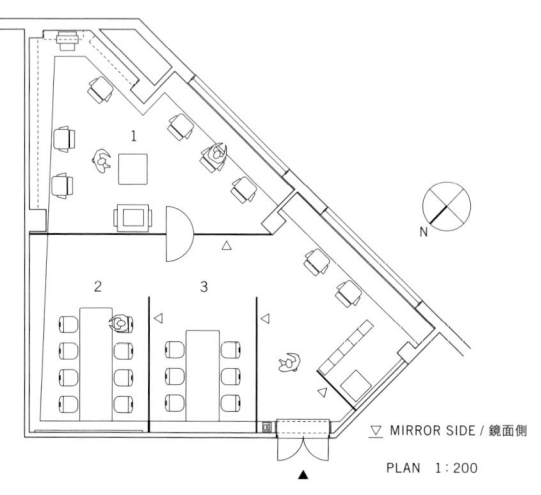

1 WORKSPACE
2 MEETING SPACE 1
3 MEETING SPACE 2

1 執務スペース
2 ミーティングスペース 1
3 ミーティングスペース 2

▽ MIRROR SIDE / 鏡面側

PLAN 1:200

P.130 DWJ Office
DWJ Office

Principle use: OFFICE
Design: Koichi Suzuno +
Shinya Kamuro + Yuho Miyai
Lighting design: MAXRAY
Construction: ASAHI BUILDING-WALL
Project management: INTERARM
Building site: Nakameguro Tokyo
Total floor area: 962.4m²
Design period: 2007.09–11
Construction period: 2007.11–12

主要用途：オフィス
設計担当：鈴野浩一＋禿 真哉＋宮井裕穂
照明計画：マックスレイ
施工：旭ビルウォール
プロジェクトマネージメント：
インターアーム
所在：東京 中目黒
延床面積：962.4㎡
設計期間：2007.09–11
施工期間：2007.11–12

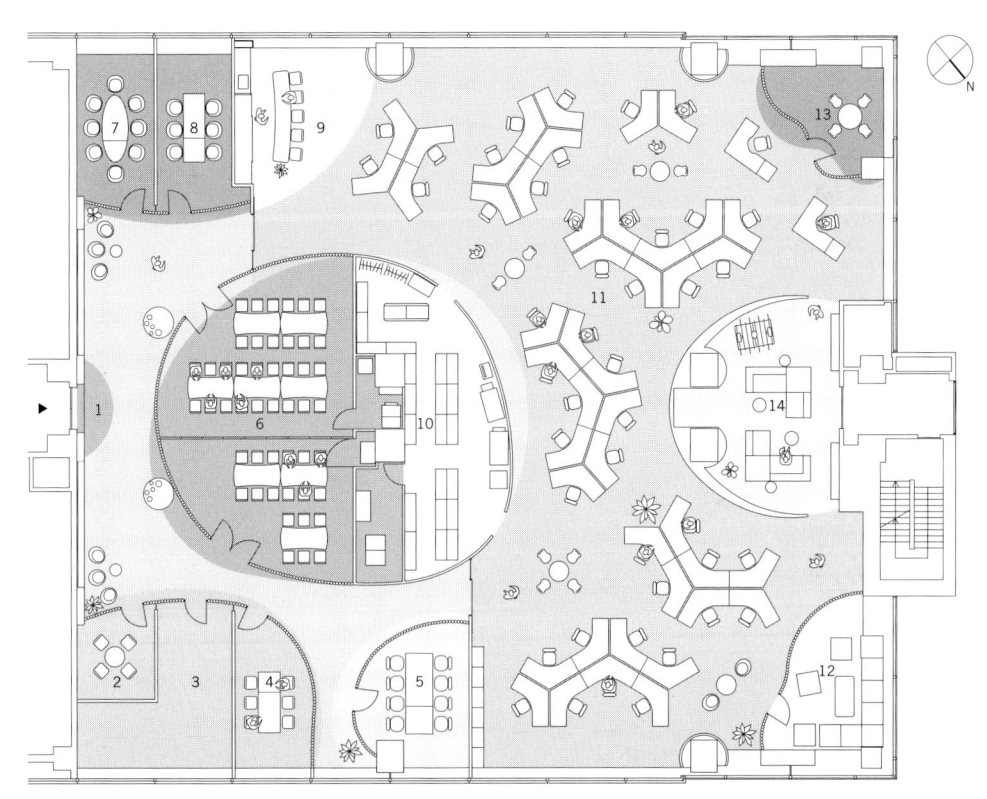

PLAN 1:300

1 LOBBY
2 MEETING ROOM 1
3 WORKSPACE 1
4 MEETING ROOM 2
5 MEETING ROOM 3
6 MEETING ROOM 4
7 MEETING ROOM 5
8 MEETING ROOM 6
9 BAR
10 UTILITY SPACE
11 WORKSPACE 2
12 MEETING ROOM 7
13 MEETING ROOM 8
14 LOUNGE

1 ロビー
2 会議室 1
3 執務スペース 1
4 会議室 2
5 会議室 3
6 会議室 4
7 会議室 5
8 会議室 6
9 バー
10 ユーティリティスペース
11 執務スペース 2
12 会議室 7
13 会議室 8
14 ラウンジ

TORAFU ARCHITECTS IDEA + PROCESS 2004-2011

P.140 Run Pit by au Smart Sports
Run Pit by au Smart Sports

Principle use: FACILITY SPACE
Design: Koichi Suzuno +
Shinya Kamuro + Eikichi Saku
Lighting design: On&Off
Construction: TAKENAKA / ISHIMARU
Planning & Producer:
Hakuhodo Experience Design
Project management:
FCI Design and Management

Signage design: TAKAIYAMA inc.
Fabric design: NUNO
Furniture: inter office
Building site: PALACESIDE BUILDING
Total floor area: 217.8m²
Design period: 2010.02-05
Construction period: 2010.05-06

主要用途：貸ロッカー／シャワー施設
設計担当：鈴野浩一＋禿 真哉＋朔 永吉
照明計画：On&Off
施工：竹中工務店／イシマル
企画・プロデュース：
博報堂エクスペリエンスデザイン
プロジェクトマネージメント：
FCIデザインアンドマネジメント

サイン計画：高い山
ファブリック：NUNO
家具：インターオフィス
所在・会場：パレスサイドビル
延床面積：217.8㎡
設計期間：2010.02-05
施工期間：2010.05-06

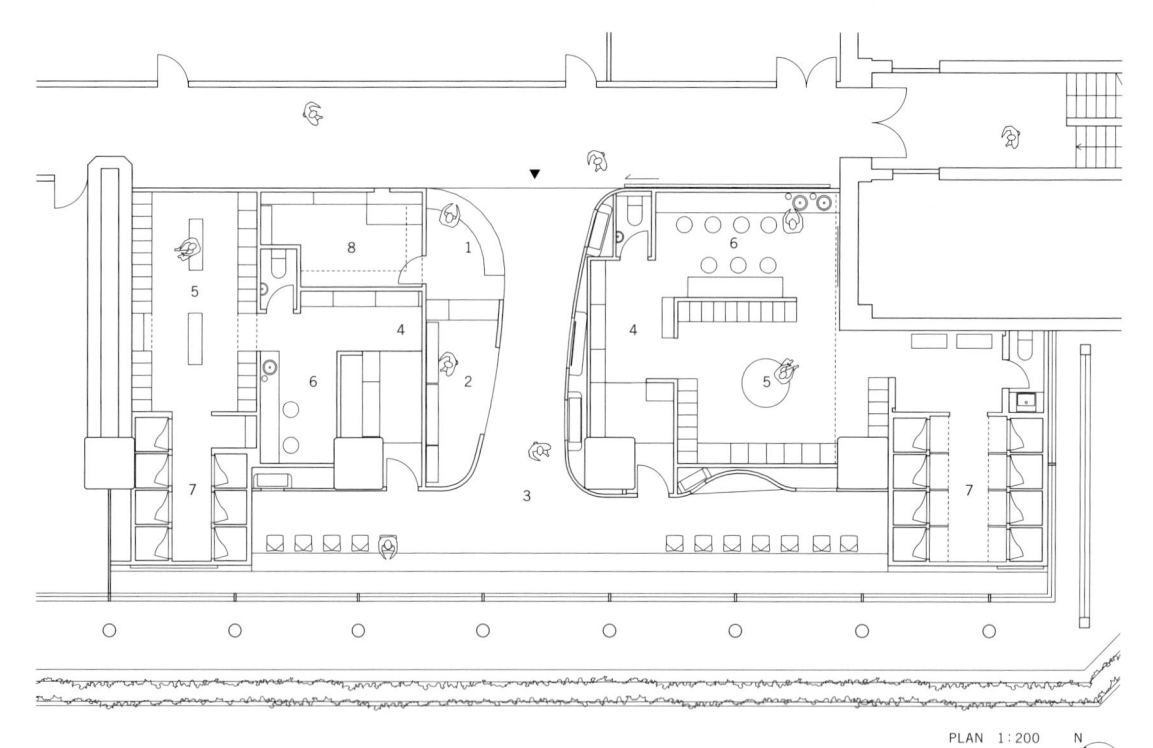

1 RECEPTION · CASHIER	1 受付・レジカウンター	
2 SHOP	2 物販コーナー	
3 FREE SPACE	3 フリースペース	
4 FOOTWEAR SPACE	4 下足スペース	
5 LOCKER SPACE	5 ロッカースペース	
6 POWDER ROOM	6 パウダースペース	
7 SHOWER SPACE	7 シャワースペース	
8 STAFF ROOM	8 スタッフルーム	

PLAN 1:200 N

1 Run Pit   1 Run Pit
2 Running Course 2 ランニングコース
3 Imperial Palace 3 皇居

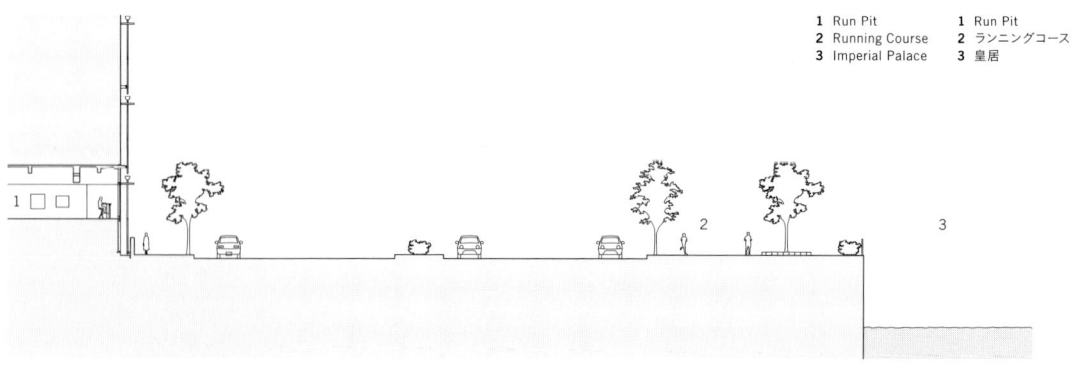

SECTION 1:700

PROJECT DATA + DRAWINGS

P.146 INHABITANT STORE TOKYO
INHABITANT STORE TOKYO

Principle use: SHOP
Design: Koichi Suzuno +
Shinya Kamuro + Tomohiko Tashiro
Lighting design: spangle
Construction: ISHIMARU
Art work: Asao Tokolo
Building site: Harajuku Tokyo
Total floor area: 224.5m²
Design period: 2009.05–08
Construction period: 2009.08–09

主要用途：物販店舗
設計担当：鈴野浩一＋禿 真哉＋田代朋彦
照明計画：スパンコール
施工：イシマル
アートワーク：野老朝雄
所在：東京 原宿
延床面積：224.5㎡
設計期間：2009.05–08
施工期間：2009.08–09

1 CASHIER
2 SHOP
3 FITTING ROOM
4 DISPLAY SPACE
5 STORAGE
6 PRESS ROOM

1 レジカウンター
2 売場
3 フィッティングルーム
4 ディスプレイスペース
5 倉庫
6 プレスルーム

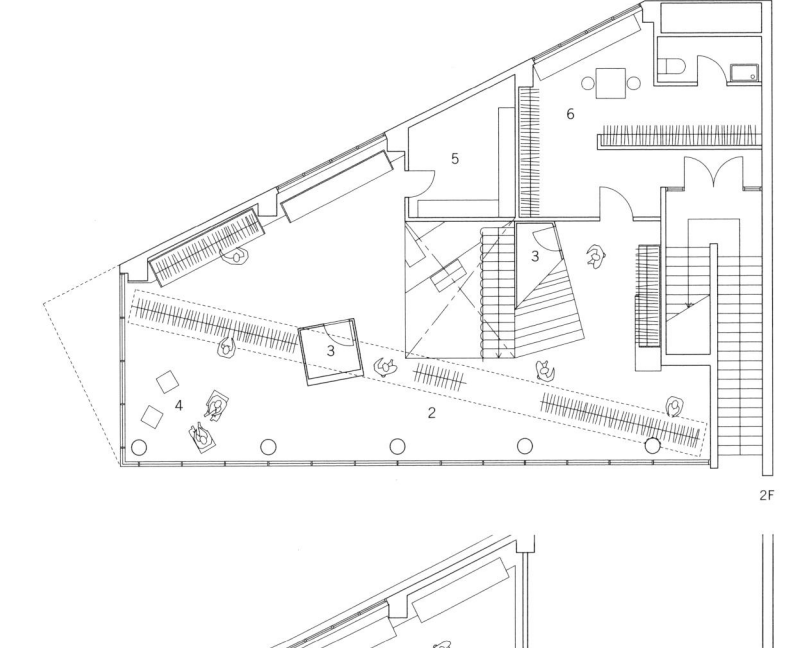

2F

1F PLAN 1:200

P.150
EXHIBITION
LIFE AND LIGHTING
くらしとあかり展

Principle use: EXHIBITED WORK
Design: Koichi Suzuno +
Shinya Kamuro + Risa Murakami
Lighting design: spangle
Construction: INOUE INDUSTRIES
Planning:
Tomoharu Makabe (M・T・VISIONS)
Building site:
ENDO Lighting Aoyama Showroom 5F
Total floor area: 117m²
Design period: 2007.08–11
Construction period: 2007.11.03
Duration: 2007.11.05–09

主要用途：展覧会作品
設計担当：鈴野浩一＋禿 真哉＋村上里砂
照明計画：スパンコール
施工：イノウエインダストリィズ
企画：真壁智治（M・T・VISIONS）
会場：遠藤照明青山ショールーム5F
延床面積：117㎡
設計期間：2007.08–11
施工期間：2007.11.03
会期：2007.11.05–09

P.152
EXHIBITION
"minä perhonen + torafu new / study"
ミナ ペルホネンとトラフの新作／習作

Principle use: PRODUCT
Design: Koichi Suzuno +
Shinya Kamuro + Hanae Yamaguchi
Production: INOUE INDUSTRIES
Design collaboration: minä perhonen
Building site:
CLASKA Gallery & Shop "DO"
Design period: 2009.06–12
Production period: 2009.11–12
Duration: 2009.12.17–2010.01.31

主要用途：プロダクト
設計担当：鈴野浩一＋禿 真哉＋山口英恵
製作：イノウエインダストリィズ
共同設計：ミナ ペルホネン
会場：クラスカ Gallery & Shop "DO"
設計期間：2009.06–12
製作期間：2009.11–12
会期：2009.12.17–2010.01.31

P.156
CHELFITSCH
"FREETIME"
チェルフィッチュ「フリータイム」

Principle use: STAGE SET
Design: Koichi Suzuno +
Shinya Kamuro + Risa Murakami
Construction: Tokyo Studio
Planning & Stage production: Precog
Building site: SuperDeluxe
Total floor area: 47.6m²
Design period: 2007.11–2008.03
Construction period: 2008.03
Duration: 2008.03.05–18

主要用途：舞台美術
設計担当：鈴野浩一＋禿 真哉＋村上里砂
施工：東京スタデオ
企画・制作：プリコグ
会場：スーパー・デラックス
延床面積：47.6㎡
設計期間：2007.11–2008.03
施工期間：2008.03
会期：2008.03.05–18

P.158 TABLE ON THE ROOF
テーブル オン ザ ルーフ

Principle use: EVENT SPACE
Design:
Koichi Suzuno + Shinya Kamuro
Lighting design: MAXRAY
Construction: cosmos more / IKEYA
Building site: Hotel CLASKA Rooftop
Total floor area: 240m²
Design period: 2004.06–08
Construction period: 2004.07–09

主要用途:多目的スペース
設計担当:鈴野浩一＋禿 真哉
照明計画:マックスレイ
施工:コスモスモア／IKEYA
所在:ホテル クラスカ 屋上
延床面積:240m²
設計期間:2004.06–08
施工期間:2004.07–09

1 TABLE
2 BAR
3 OFFICE

1 テーブル
2 バーカウンター
3 オフィス

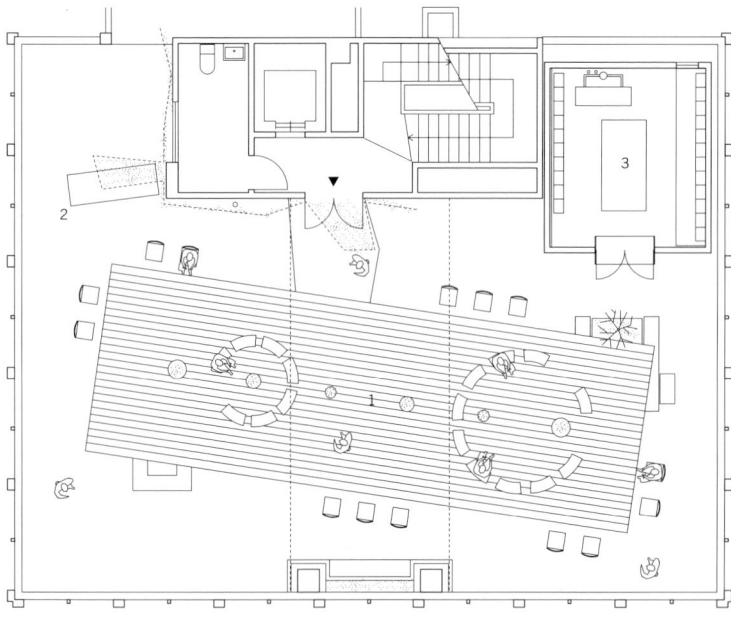

P.162 Deck
デッキ

Principle use: PRODUCT
Design: Koichi Suzuno +
Shinya Kamuro + Kazunori Arihara
Material: Decking
Size: W70 × D500 × H360mm
Building site:
NAMURA Osaka (DESIGNEAST)
Design period: 2010.09
Duration: 2010.10.01–03

主要用途:プロダクト
設計担当:鈴野浩一＋禿 真哉＋有原寿典
素材:デッキ材
サイズ:W70×D500×H360㎜
会場:
大阪 名村造船所跡地 (DESIGNEAST)
設計期間:2010.09
会期:2010.10.01–03

PLAN 1:200

P.164 BOOLEAN (Tokyo University Tetsumon Cafe)
ブーリアン (東京大学医学部教育研究棟 鉄門カフェ)

Principle use: CAFE
Design:
Koichi Suzuno + Shinya Kamuro
Lighting design: MAXRAY
Construction: INOUE INDUSTRIES
Building site: The University of Tokyo
Faculty of Medicine Experimental
Research Building 1F
Total floor area: 48m²
Design period: 2006.06–2007.01
Construction period: 2007.02–03

主要用途:カフェ
設計担当:鈴野浩一＋禿 真哉
照明計画:マックスレイ
施工:イノウエインダストリィズ
所在:東京大学医学部教育研究棟1階
延床面積:48㎡
設計期間:2006.06–2007.01
施工期間:2007.02–03

1 TERRACE
2 CAFE
3 KITCHEN

1 テラス
2 カフェ
3 キッチン

212

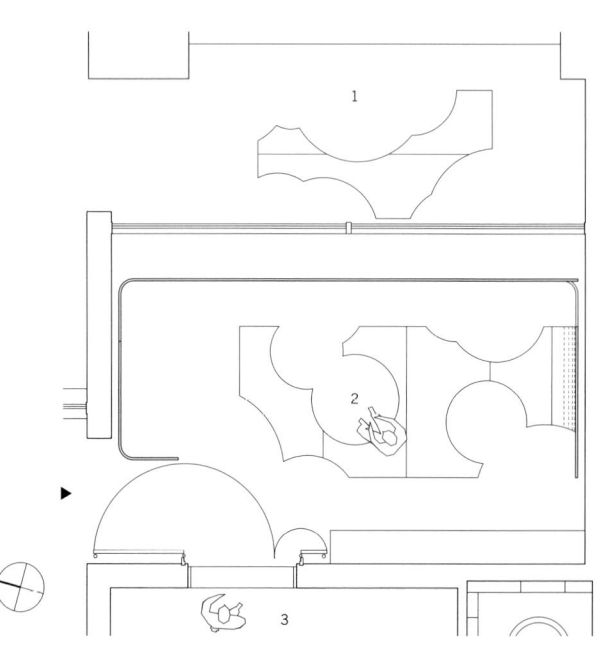

PLAN 1:100

PROJECT DATA + DRAWINGS

P.168 EXHIBITION "bones"
「骨」展

Principle use: EXHIBITION SITE
Design: Koichi Suzuno +
Shinya Kamuro + Rui Igarashi
Lighting design: MAXRAY
Construction: Zeal Associate
Signage design: TAKAIYAMA inc.
Building site: 21_21 DESIGN SIGHT
Total floor area: 1226m²
Design period: 2008.05–2009.04
Construction period: 2009.05
Duration: 2009.05.29–08.30

主要用途：展示会場構成
設計担当：鈴野浩一＋禿 真哉＋
五十嵐瑠衣
照明計画：マックスレイ
施工：ジールアソシエイツ
サイン計画：高い山
会場：21_21 DESIGN SIGHT
延床面積：1226㎡
設計期間：2008.05–2009.04
施工期間：2009.05
会期：2009.05.29–08.30

P.172 HOUSE IN INOKASHIRA
井の頭の住宅

Principle use: HOUSE
Design:
Koichi Suzuno + Shinya Kamuro
Construction: TANAKA / TSUKI-ZO
Building site: Mitaka Tokyo
Total floor area: 75.3m²
Design period: 2005.02–05
Construction period: 2005.06–08

主要用途：住宅
設計担当：鈴野浩一＋禿 真哉
施工：田中建設／月造
所在：東京 三鷹
延床面積：75.3㎡
設計期間：2005.02–05
施工期間：2005.06–08

P.174 RING PARKING
リング パーキング

Principle use: PARKING
Design:
Koichi Suzuno + Shinya Kamuro + Naofumi Nanba
Construction: TSUKI-ZO
Building site: Kawasaki Kanagawa
Total floor area: 90m²
Design period: 2006.07–10
Construction period: 2006.11

主要用途：駐輪場
設計担当：鈴野浩一＋禿 真哉＋難波真史
施工：月造
所在：神奈川 川崎
延床面積：90㎡
設計期間：2006.07–10
施工期間：2006.11

P.176 KIRIKO BOTTLE
キリコ ボトル

Principle use: PRODUCT
Design:
Koichi Suzuno + Shinya Kamuro
Production: Tadayuki Ohkubo
Material: Glass
Design period: 2006.07–2007.01
Production period: 2007.02–03

主要用途：プロダクト
設計担当：鈴野浩一＋禿 真哉
製作：大久保忠幸
素材：ガラス
設計期間：2006.07–2007.01
製作期間：2007.02–03

P.177 CMYK
CMYK

Principle use: PRODUCT
Design:
Koichi Suzuno + Shinya Kamuro
Production: SFIDA
Material:
PU synthetic leather / Butyl tube
Size:
Football size 4 (Diameter φ200mm)
Design period: 2008.07–10
Production period: 2008.10–12

主要用途：プロダクト
設計担当：鈴野浩一＋禿 真哉
製作：SFIDA
素材：PU合成皮革／ブチルチューブ
サイズ：4号球（直径 φ200mm）
設計期間：2008.07–10
製作期間：2008.10–12

P.178 tapehook
tapehook

Principle use: PRODUCT
Design: Koichi Suzuno +
Shinya Kamuro + Akira Yamage
Production: Kami no Kousakujo
Package Design: TAKAIYAMA inc.
Material: Paper
Size: W15×D17×H45mm
Design period: 2010.11–2011.02
Production period: 2011.02–04

主要用途：プロダクト
設計担当：鈴野浩一＋禿 真哉＋山家 明
製作：かみの工作所
パッケージデザイン：高い山
素材：紙
サイズ：W15×D17×H45mm
設計期間：2010.11–2011.02
製作期間：2011.02–04

P.180 airvase
空気の器

Principle use: PRODUCT
Design: Koichi Suzuno +
Shinya Kamuro + Hisamichi Iizuka
Production: Kami no Kousakujo
Package Design: TAKAIYAMA inc.
Material: Paper
Size: Bowl Diameter φ193mm
Design period: 2009.10–12
Production period:
2009.12–2010.01

主要用途：プロダクト
設計担当：鈴野浩一＋禿 真哉＋飯塚之道
製作：かみの工作所
パッケージデザイン：高い山
素材：紙
サイズ：器 直径 φ193mm
設計期間：2009.10–12
製作期間：2009.12–2010.01

TORAFU ARCHITECTS IDEA + PROCESS 2004-2011

PROFILE

TORAFU ARCHITECTS
トラフ建築設計事務所

Founded in 2004 by Koichi Suzuno (right) and Shinya Kamuro (left), TORAFU ARCHITECTS employs a working approach based on architectural thinking. Works by the duo include a diverse range of products, from architectural design to interior design for shops, exhibition space design, product design, spatial installations and film making. They have received many prizes including the Design for Asia (DFA) Grand Award for the "TEMPLATE IN CLASKA" in 2005, and the Grand Prize of the Elita Design Awards 2011 with "Light Loom (Milano Salone 2011)". The *airvase book* was published in 2011.

鈴野浩一(右)と禿真哉(左)により2004年に設立。建築の設計をはじめ、ショップのインテリアデザイン、展覧会の会場構成、プロダクトデザイン、空間インスタレーションやムービー制作への参加など多岐に渡り、建築的な思考をベースに取り組んでいる。「テンプレート イン クラスカ」で2005アジアデザインアワード大賞、「光の織機(Canon Milano Salone 2011)」でELITA DESIGN AWARDS 2011 最優秀賞など多数受賞。2011年『空気の器の本』(美術出版社)を刊行。

STAFF
Koichi Suzuno / 鈴野浩一
Shinya Kamuro / 禿 真哉

Tomohiko Tashiro / 田代朋彦
Eikichi Saku / 朔 永吉
Hanae Yamaguchi / 山口英恵
Hisamichi Iizuka / 飯塚之通
Akira Yamage / 山家 明
Kazunori Arihara / 有原寿典
Jody Wong / ジョディ・ウォン

FORMER STAFF / 元所員
Yuho Miyai / 宮井裕穂
Naofumi Nanba / 難波真史
Ritsuko Ameno / 飴野りつ子
Risa Murakami / 村上里砂
Naohiro Nakamura / 中村尚弘
Rui Igarashi / 五十嵐瑠衣

2011年5月現在

www.torafu.com

PHOTOGRAPHY CREDITS / 撮影クレジット

Madoka Akiyama / 秋山まどか
162

Daici Ano / 阿野太一
2-3, 15, 18, 19, 20, 21, 22, 23左下, 24-25, 26, 27, 34, 35, 44-45, 46, 47, 48, 49, 51, 52-53, 54, 55, 56, 57右下, 60下, 64-65, 66, 67右上, 67右上, 67右下, 72, 73, 74, 76, 77, 78, 88, 89, 90, 91, 92, 93, 94, 95, 96, 97, 102, 103, 104, 105, 106, 107, 108, 109左, 112-113, 114, 115, 116, 117, 118, 120, 121, 122, 123上, 124, 125, 126-127, 129, 130, 131, 132, 133上, 134下, 136上, 140-141, 142, 143, 144, 145, 146, 147, 148, 149, 164, 165, 166, 167上, 172, 173上

Ryoukan Abe / 阿部良寛
176

Masanori Ikeda / 池田昌紀
134上, 188, 189, 214, 215

Takayuki Izumi / 和泉孝之
150, 151

Daisuke Ohki / 大木大輔
10左列2段目, 58-59, 61, 62, 63左上, 63右上

Takumi Ota / 太田拓実
28, 29, 30-31, 40-41, 42, 100左下, 101, 177

Hiroshi Koike / 小池博史
32-33

Rokusuke Sakurai / 桜井ロクスケ
171

Daisuke Shimokawa (Nacasa & Partners) /
下川大輔 (Nacasa & Partners)
60上, 98-99, 100左上, 100右上

Shinkenchiku-sha / 新建築社
14, 16, 110左上, 110右上, 160上

Kenshu Shintsubo / 新津保建秀
152, 153

Chiyoe Sugita / 杉田知洋江
155

Satomi Tomita / 冨田里美
180, 181上

Nobuaki Nakagawa / 中川敦玲
68-69, 70, 136下, 158-159, 160左下, 160右下, 161左上, 161右上

Hiroyuki Hirai / 平井広行
137中

Toru Yokota / 横田徹
156, 157

Fuminari Yoshitsugu / 吉次史成
36, 37, 38, 39, 178, 179, 181左下, 182, 183, 184

Masaya Yoshimura / 吉村昌也
168-169, 170

Shinichi Watanabe / 渡辺慎一
174, 175上

Unless otherwise credited above,
all photographs are by TORAFU ARCHITECTS

上記以外の写真はすべて、トラフ建築設計事務所提供

TORAFU ARCHITECTS
IDEA + PROCESS
2004-2011

トラフ建築設計事務所のアイデアとプロセス

First published 2011

2011年6月6日 初版発行

Author: TORAFU ARCHITECTS
Design: Hideyuki Yamano, Kohei Sekida and Kyoko Tanaka (TAKAYAMA inc.)
Editorial Cooperation: Hiroki Shinkawa
Translation: Katsutoshi Kawamata
Printing: Kyodo Printing
Printed in Japan
ISBN978-4-568-60039-1 C3052

Bijutsu Shuppan Sha Co., Ltd.
Jimbocho Place 9F, Kanda-jimbocho,
Chiyoda-ku, Tokyo, 101-8417, Japan
www.bijutsu.co.jp/bss/

著　者　トラフ建築設計事務所
デザイン　山野英之＋関田浩平＋田中恭子 (高い山)
編集協力　新川博己
翻　訳　川又勝利
編　集　宮後優子、保田美樹子 (美術出版社)
印刷製本　共同印刷 (製版：田川 睦)

発行人　大下健太郎
発　行　株式会社美術出版社
　　　　〒101-8417
　　　　東京都千代田区神田神保町3-2-3 神保町プレイス9F
　　　　TEL. 03-3235-5136 [営業] 03-3234-2173 [編集]
　　　　振替 00130-3-447800
　　　　www.bijutsu.co.jp/bss/

©TORAFU ARCHITECTS Printed in Japan
ISBN978-4-568-60039-1 C3052
All rights reserved. No part of this publication may be reproduced.

©TORAFU ARCHITECTS Printed in Japan
ISBN978-4-568-60039-1 C3052
本書の全部または一部を無断で複写複製 (コピー) することを禁じます。